★ WEAPONS OF WAR
TANKS AND ARMORED VEHICLES
1900–1945

★ WEAPONS OF WAR
TANKS AND ARMORED VEHICLES
1900–1945

CHARTWELL
BOOKS, INC.

CHARTWELL BOOKS, INC.
A division of BOOK SALES, INC.
276 Fifth Avenue Suite 206
New York, New York 10001
USA

© 2013 by Amber Books Ltd

Contributing authors: Chris Chant, Steve Crawford, Martin J. Dougherty, Ian Hogg,
Robert Jackson, Chris McNab, Michael Sharpe, Philip Trewhitt

ISBN 978-0-7858-2997-3

Printed in China

PICTURE CREDITS
Photographs:
Art-Tech/Aerospace: 8–10, 14–17
Art-Tech/MARS: 18
Cody Images: 6, 7, 19–21, 23
Personal Archives of Bonalume Ricardo Neto: 11, 12/13, 22

Ilustrations: © Art-Tech/Aerospace

CONTENTS

Introduction

Tanks and AFVs

The advent of the tank and armoured fighting vehicle fundametally changed the basis of early twentieth-century warfare.

While Main Battle Tanks often capture the attention of media and enthusiasts, their role on the modern battlefield is actually a rather minor one. For of all the factors which contribute to combat success, vehicle logistics always ranks amongst the most important. Without the ability to transport men and material from the industrial base to the actual frontline, an army will be starved of the means to prosecute war.

THE YEARS OF EXPERIMENTATION

World War I began the true mechanization of logistics and infantry manoeuvres. Three particular needs arose. The first was to transport the vast amounts of ammunition required for conducting artillery warfare.

TANK MK V: see page 118

FT-17: see page 114

Second, trench warfare demanded a constant influx of supplies to maintain the viability of the static positions. Finally, in the last years of the war, tacticians sought ways to speed up assault manoeuvres across no-man's land and reduce high-volume casualties.

None of these problems were adequately solved during the war. Yet the conflict served to challenge the military's outdated ideas of horse-drawn transport towards new conceptions of mechanized logistics and combat.

More and more countries developed armoured cars: France the Laffly-White, Germany the A5P and the Daimler/15, Italy the

Autoblinda IZ, Russia the Garford-Putilow, and the UK 'Little Willie', the forerunner of the first tanks. Apart from this latter example, most armoured vehicles of World War I were simply civilian machines clad in crude iron and armed with a machine-gun or cannon. Their performance was frequently poor, with top speeds of around 45km/h (28mph) and a limited ability to negotiate the muddy conditions that characterized the Western and Eastern fronts. In addition, industry was not geared up to the mass-production methods required to equip large-scale armies. Consequently the impact of armoured cars on infantry warfare was minimal, though

PANZER I: see page 122

they did find good use as urban security and patrol vehicles where road conditions were less demanding.

TRUCKS

Trucks also made an appearance in World War I, though mainly in the form of requisitioned civilian vehicles. Some 825 civilian trucks were put into military service by Germany during the conflict, with 3000 tractors, 7700 heavy trucks and 50,000 cars in reserve. (German citizens received grants and annual subsidies for purchasing a truck, the agreement being that the truck would be requisitioned by the army if necessary.)

Four-wheel-drive US trucks manufactured by FWD Corporation entered service on the Western front in 1917. Yet the trucks still did not have the capability or numbers to threaten horse-drawn logistics. Of greater persuasion were the tracked vehicles entering service. Tracked transporters, in spite of their persistent unreliability, slow speed and inadequate weaponry, demonstrated that vehicles could go where horses couldn't and transport far greater loads. The Renault Cargo Carrier of 1916 only moved at 6.5km/h (4mph) but had a cargo capacity of 4 or 5 tons. In 1918, the US Holt Tractor, Caisson Mk VII carried

PANZER IV: see page 134

Tanks were first used decisively in the Allied victory at Amiens in August 1918.

five tons at 11.2km/h (7mph). American designers also elongated British Mk V tanks to create a troop compartment for a squad of soldiers – and the first true Armoured Personnel Carrier (APC) was born.

FIRST BLOOD

On 8 August 1918, a British force of 414 combat tanks and 120 supply tanks, supported by 800 aircraft, played a key role in the decisive Allied victory at Amiens. The

impression was given that a true revolution in military technology had occurred that would change the face of warfare forever. The events of the next few months would show that Amiens had been a false dawn and that it would be another 20 years before technology caught up with the theories of visionaries such as J.F.C. Fuller, who devised the futuristic Plan 1919. The process of creating the tanks and other essential equipment that would transform the theory and practice of armoured warfare between 1939 and 1945 was to be long and hard.

World War I ended not with a mechanization of warfare, but at least mechanized progress. During the interwar period tacticians such as Major-General J.F.C. Fuller in the UK and the German army officer Heinz Guderian propounded the mechanization of war as the key way to seize military advantage. The full mechanization of armies was still too much of a cultural change for many nations, Germany later being an exception, but vehicular technology was advancing. Far better engines, suspension systems, and armaments were developed, improving both the off-road mobility and combat performance of military vehicles. More investment was poured into vehicle technologies and by World War II mechanized warfare became a reality.

Although US and French armoured forces soon came under infantry control, in Britain the Tank Corps just retained its independence. Most importantly, in 1923 it also managed to acquire a modern tank, the Vickers Medium. Whilst the design had many faults, it was able to serve as a test-bed for establishing which of the many theories of

MATILDA II: see page 132

M3 STUART: see page 145

M4 SHERMAN: see page 149

WEAPONS OF WAR

T-34: see page 139

The 'big wheel' supension system offered huge improvements in cross-country performance for many tanks.

armoured warfare were truly practical. The most important trials were the exercises carried out in 1927–31 by the Experimental Mechanized Force, which pioneered the techniques of tanks, artillery, infantry and engineers all operating together under radio control.

RADIO TECHNOLOGY

The development of reliable radio was arguably one of the most significant technological advances affecting armoured warfare in the interwar years, but improved weapons, engines, tracks and suspension systems were also vital in allowing theories to be transformed into reality. Possibly the greatest innovator of the period was an eccentric American inventor, J. Walter Christie, who devised a variety of amphibious and airmobile tanks.

Whilst these projects were asking too much of the technology of the time, his 'big wheel' suspension system, soon to be known as the Christie suspension, offered an immense improvement in cross-country performance and was adopted for a host of British and Soviet tank designs, including the Crusader, Cromwell and T-34.

French designers pioneered the use of very large castings for gun mantlets, turrets and eventually entire tank hulls, a technique also taken up by the US and Soviet Union and, to a lesser extent, the UK. Most early tanks had used riveted or bolted armour, which was inherently dangerous as hostile fire could shear off the rivets and bolts, which became lethal projectiles flying around inside the vehicle. Welding overcame this vulnerability, although the welds had to be subjected to stringent quality control to

PANTHER: see page 152

CHURCHILL: see page 142

WEAPONS OF WAR

TIGER I see page 151

World War II led to a huge expansion of mechanized warfare and the development of many new types of AFVs.

ensure they could withstand hits from high--velocity weapons.

The inter-war years were also marked by significant improvements in weapons technology as the machine guns and low-velocity guns of World War I gradually gave way to high-velocity weapons capable of destroying tanks at ranges out to 1km (0.6 miles) or more. Even so, the chances of acquiring and

hitting a target at that sort of range remained minimal until well into the war.

MULTI-PURPOSE VEHICLES

World War II is significant in the story of the mechanization of warfare for two main reasons. First, the range of what constituted 'military vehicles' broadened massively to include specialist machines such as radio

New types of basic armoured personnel carriers provided the basis for a wide range of infantry fighting vehicles.

vehicles, command vehicles, engineer vehicles and self-propelled guns. Second, the quantities of vehicles available made the mechanization of large-scale units possible. These two factors were decisive.

During the war, multi-purpose vehicles became common, vehicles which took a standard format as the basis for several spe-cialist roles. Halftracks, a particular pheno-menon of the conflict, were ideally suited for this flexibility, being manoeuvrable, durable and offering troop- and cargo-carrying capa-city. The German SdKfz 250, for example, was not only a basic APC but also converted to a communications vehicle (SdKfz 250/2 and 3), a mortar platform (SdKfz 250/7),

SDKFZ 234: see page 59

BREN GUN CARRIER: see page 69

a self-propelled anti-tank system (SdKfz 250/9), an anti-tank gun carrier (SdKfz 250/8) and a range-finding and artillery survey vehicle (SdKfz 250/12) amongst others.

Trucks became more dependable and capable in World War II, and improved techniques of mass production ensured they were available in sufficient numbers. Horse carriage, though still heavily used, was the transport of default, not of choice. A British 6x4 Leyland Hippo truck could carry 10 tons of cargo at speeds of around 64km/h (40mph) for a distance of 837km (520 miles), a feat well beyond the easy capacity of horse logistics. Each side built up fleets of trucks and made them an intrinsic part of infantry battalions and armoured units.

ENGINEERING VEHICLES

With the increase in mechanization came an expansion in engineering challenges for the wartime armies, and multifarious engineer vehicles were developed. The Sherman Beach Armoured Recovery Vehicle (BARV) was created from a turretless Sherman tank for the purpose of towing stuck vehicles from

M3 HALFTRACK see page 80

GMC 6X6: see page 162

World War II also led to the rise of amphibious vehicles, such as the US-made DUKW and the German Schwimmwagen.

deep water or soft sand during amphibious operations. Churchill tanks were mounted with fascine and mat-laying devices to create mobile road-laying or ditch-breaching machines. In Germany, the massive railway-mounted Karl 600mm (23.62in) mortar required a specialist ammunition carrier to transport its 2-ton shells. The result was the Munitionstransporter IV, based on the chassis of the PzKpfw IV Ausf F tank but fitted with a 3000kg (6614lb) capacity crane and racks to carry four shells. The list could go on, but mobile engineering vehicles became a necessary presence for all sides

during the war, and helped to keep fleets of vehicles in action.

AMPHIBIOUS VEHICLES

Another interesting development in World War II was the rise of amphibious vehicles. These offered many manoeuvre advantages, the principal being that they did not require the assistance of another vehicle or unit to transport their cargo from the water to an inland position. They usually fell into three categories of use: beach assault vehicle, reconnaissance vehicle and APC. The American DUKW – affectionately known as

JEEP: see page 93

SCHWIMMWAGEN: see page 27

By the close of World War II, mechanization had become essential for the functioning of a modern army.

the 'Duck' – was the most famous of the first category, able to carry either a sizeable unit of troops or five tons of cargo from sea to beach at speeds of 9.7km/h (6mph). In the Pacific conflict, experience of aggressive amphibious landings on Japanese-occupied islands led to the development of the US LVT series of vehicles, designed to provide combat influence rather than just cargo-landing. The LVT(A) 1, for example, was fully turreted and armed with a heavy machine gun and a 37mm (1.45in) cannon for immediate beachhead fire support.

The list of vehicle innovations in World War II could go on and on, but when the war ended a key change had occurred in the nature of modern armies. Mechanization had

become essential rather than preferred. As the world entered the Cold War, units had to be fully mechanized to meet the greater speed and mobility of armed conflict. This was assisted by the reduction in size of most armies following World War II, but that reduction in size meant that survivability had to depend on speed and defensive techno-logy rather than physical numbers of troops. The Cold War period did little to change the basic categories of military vehicles. What it did transform, however, was their fighting capability.

When World War II ended a key chan-ge had occurred in the nature of modern armies. Mechanization had become essential rather than preferred.

Vickers-Carden-Loyd Type 31

The Vickers-Carden-Loyd amphibious vehicle was the brainchild of J.V. Carden and V. Loyd, employees of the British Vickers works. During the late 1920s, they designed a series of light tanks for the British Army, one of which became the Vickers-Carden-Loyd Type 31; the world's first operational amphibious tank. The Type 31 was basically a Vickers 4-ton light tank fitted with a pontoon-shaped watertight hull. The vehicle floated by virtue of buoyant mudguards. Power came from a propeller at the rear of the hull which gave a top speed of 10km/h (6mph). Directional control was provided by a rudder. The Type 31 sold only on the export market, particularly to the Far East, and it inspired other nations to build their own.

SPECIFICATIONS

COUNTRY OF ORIGIN: United Kingdom
CREW: 2
WEIGHT: 3100kg (6834lb)
DIMENSIONS: length 3.96m (12ft 11in); width 2.08m (6ft 10in); height 1.83m (6ft)
RANGE: 260km (162 miles)
ARMOUR: (steel) 9mm (0.35in) maximum
ARMAMENT: 1 x 7.7mm (0.31in) MG
POWERPLANT: 1 x Meadows 6-cylinder petrol, developing 56hp (42kW)
PERFORMANCE: maximum road speed: 64km/h (39mph); maximum water speed: 10km/h (6mph)

T-37

The origins of the T-37 are to be found in the 1931 purchase by the Soviet Union of a number of British Carden-Loyd amphibious tanks. The Soviets were duly impressed but realized that the tank was unsuited to fulfil all their requirements. Their version of the British design eventually became the T-37. The first production models appeared in late 1933. A small vehicle with a crew of just two, their buoyancy stemmed from pontoons attached to either side of the hull. Designed mainly for reconnaissance, and with only light armour and armament, they nevertheless were used in a combat role following the German invasion in 1941, where they fared badly and were replaced as quickly as possible. A few were retained for use as light tractors.

SPECIFICATIONS

COUNTRY OF ORIGIN: Soviet Union
CREW: 2
WEIGHT: 3200kg (7055lb)
DIMENSIONS: length 3.75m (12ft 4in); width 2.10m (6ft 11in); height 1.82m (5ft 11in)
RANGE: 185km (115 miles)
ARMOUR: 3–9mm (0.1–0.4in)
ARMAMENT: 1 x 7.62mm (0.3in) machine gun
POWERPLANT: 1 x GAZ AA petrol engine developing 40hp (29.8kW)
PERFORMANCE: maximum speed 56.3km/h (35mph); fording amphibious; vertical obstacle 0.79m (2ft 7in); trench 1.88m (6ft 2in)

Land-Wasser-Schlepper

In 1936, the German Army contracted Rheimetall to build a special tractor for amphibious operations, which could tow behind it a cargo trailer also capable of floating. The Land-Wasser-Schlepper was essentially a motor tug fitted with tracks, capable of carrying up to 20 passengers. Its ungainly appearance belied its effective performance. However, it was rather cumbersome on land and suffered from a lack of armour. Even though designed for the calm waters of inland Europe, the project was pursued with enthusiasm while the invasion of England looked possible. After this was cancelled, interest waned and the project was cancelled in turn. Nevertheless, a pre-production series of seven vehicles was produced and some of them went on to serve on the Eastern Front after 1941.

SPECIFICATIONS

COUNTRY OF ORIGIN: Germany
CREW: 3 + 20
WEIGHT: 13,000kg (28,660lb)
DIMENSIONS: length 8.60m (28ft 3in); width 3.16m (10ft 4in); height 3.13m (10ft 3in)
RANGE: 240km (149 miles)
ARMOUR: unknown
ARMAMENT: none
POWERPLANT: 1 x Maybach HL 120 TRM V-12 engine developing 265hp (197.6kW)
PERFORMANCE: maximum road speed 40km/h (24.85mph); maximum water speed unloaded 12.5km/h (7.8mph); fording amphibious

Schwimmwagen Type 166

The Schwimmwagen Type 166 was an amphibious light vehicle developed by Volkswagen in the early 1940s. It was meant to provide German infantry and airborne units with an amphibious version of the excellent Kübelwagen. A bulbous flotation body was added to the Kübelwagen and a chain-driven propeller (which had to be lowered prior to entering the water) situated at the rear of the hull. The front wheels acted as the rudder. With its maximum load of four men, the Schwimmwagen had an on-water speed of 11km/h (7mph). Of the 14,625 Schwimmwagens produced during World War II, most ended up serving on the Eastern Front, though small numbers went to North Africa.

SPECIFICATIONS

COUNTRY OF ORIGIN: Germany
CREW: 1 + 3
WEIGHT: 910kg (2007lb)
DIMENSIONS: length 3.82m (12ft 6in); width 1.48m (4ft 10in); height 1.61m (5ft 3in)
RANGE: 520km (323 miles)
ARMOUR: none
ARMAMENT: none
POWERPLANT: 1 x VW 4-cylinder petrol, developing 25hp (19kW)
PERFORMANCE: maximum road speed: 80km/h (50mph); maximum water speed: 11km/h (7mph)

T-40

The T-40 was designed to replace the T-37, whose manifold deficiencies had become painfully apparent by 1938. To speed development, the design included as many automobile components as possible. Flotation tanks were fitted at the rear, giving the vehicle a rather bulky appearance. The T-40 was equipped with very thin armour and fared poorly as a result during the fighting in Finland in 1939. It was thus decided to dispense with the amphibious characteristics and use the vehicle as a land tank. This proved an impractical conversion and its use was minimal after that, seeing some service with armoured formations as a reconnaissance vehicle during 1941 against the Germans. Only around 225 T-40s were ever built, as light tanks were given low priority at that time.

SPECIFICATIONS

COUNTRY OF ORIGIN: Soviet Union
CREW: 2
WEIGHT: 5900kg (12,980lb)
DIMENSIONS: length 4.11m (13ft 6in); width 2.33m (7ft 8in); height 1.95m (6ft 5in)
RANGE: 360km (224 miles)
ARMOUR: 8–14mm (0.3–0.55in)
ARMAMENT: 1 x 12.7mm (0.5in) machine gun
POWERPLANT: 1 x GAZ-202 petrol engine developing 70hp (52.2kW)
PERFORMANCE: maximum speed 44km/h (27.3mph); fording amphibious; vertical obstacle 0.70m (2ft 3.6in); trench 3.12m (10ft 3in)

DUKW

Universally known as the 'Duck', the DUKW first appeared in 1942. In essence it was a derivative of the GMC 6 x 6 truck with a boat-shaped hull for buoyancy. The simple design made it easy to operate and maintain and over 21,000 were built before the end of World War II, seeing service with all Allied forces. Designed to carry supplies from ships to the beach, it could in fact travel much farther inland, carrying troops or even light artillery. A number of weapons-carrying versions were produced, including the Scorpion, which could be used as a rocket launcher. Despite limited load-carrying capability and temperamental performance in rough seas, the DUKW was a sturdy and reliable vehicle and has often been described as an Allied war-winner.

SPECIFICATIONS

COUNTRY OF ORIGIN: United States
CREW: 2
WEIGHT: 9097kg (20,055lb)
DIMENSIONS: length 9.75m (31ft 11in); width 2.51m (8ft 3in); height 2.69m (8ft 10in)
RANGE: 120km (75 miles)
ARMOUR: none

ARMAMENT: basic version – none
POWERPLANT: 1 x GMC Model 270 engine developing 91.5hp (68.2kW)
PERFORMANCE: maximum land speed 80km/h (50mph); maximum water speed 9.7km/h (6mph); fording amphibious

Ford GPA

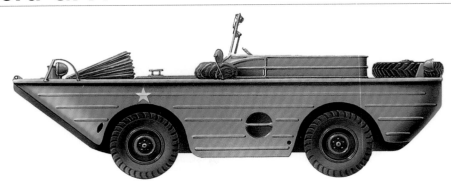

The Ford General Purpose Amphibious (GPA) had its origins in a National Defense Research Committee (NDRC) project in 1941, which sought to develop a troop-carrying amphibious vehicle. A collaborative effort by the Marmon-Herrington Company, the boat builders Sparkman & Stephens and the Ford Motor Company resulted in the Ford GPA, an amphibious version of the Willys Jeep. The GPA did not achieve the Jeep's status. Production had been rushed to meet the needs of US invasion forces in North Africa and Italy, and only 12,778 out of the 50,000 ordered were built. It was too small to be a useful seagoing craft, and most went to the Russians under the Lend-Lease agreement.

SPECIFICATIONS

COUNTRY OF ORIGIN: United States
CREW: 1 +3
WEIGHT: 1647kg (3632lb)
DIMENSIONS: length 4.62m (15ft 2in); width 1.63m (5ft 4in); height 1.73m (5ft 8in)
RANGE: not available
ARMOUR: none
ARMAMENT: none
POWERPLANT: 1 x GPA-6005 4-cylinder petrol, developing 54hp (40kW)
PERFORMANCE: maximum road speed: 105km/h (65mph); maximum water speed: 8km/h (5mph)

LVT 2

The LVT 2 was an improvement on the LVT 1, which was a civil design intended for use in the Florida swamps and not really suited for combat. The new vehicle used the engine and transmission of the M3 Light Tank. Initially the engine was mounted at the rear which restricted cargo space, but this was soon solved by moving the engine to the front in later versions. Steering and brake systems were also problematic for inexperienced crews. These vehicles were used widely in the early Pacific campaigns, from Guadalcanal onwards. They also saw action in northwest Europe during the latter stages of the war. Some versions had rocket-launchers, flame-throwers and light cannon, but their main role was to carry ashore the first wave of a landing force.

SPECIFICATIONS

COUNTRY OF ORIGIN: United States
CREW: 3
WEIGHT: 17,509kg (38,519lb)
DIMENSIONS: length 7.95m (26ft 1in); width 3.25m (10ft 8in); height 3.02m (9ft 10in)
RANGE: road radius 241km (150 miles); water radius 120.7km (75 miles)
ARMOUR: 12mm (0.47in)
ARMAMENT: 1 x 12.7mm (0.5in) and 1 x 7.62mm (0.3in) machine-guns
POWERPLANT: 2 x Cadillac petrol engines developing a total of 220hp (164.1kW)
PERFORMANCE: maximum land speed 27.3km/h (17mph); maximum water speed 9.7km/h (6mph)

Type 2 Ka-Mi

Development of the Type 2 began in the 1930s, with efforts to turn the Type 95 Kyu-Go light tank into an amphibious vehicle by adding flotation tanks. The unwieldy results prompted the designers to fit pontoons to the tank to provide buoyancy, retaining the main components of the tank. The new Type 2, as it was designated, went into production in 1942. The most commonly used Japanese amphibious tank, it contained several innovations including radio and telephone intercom system for the crew, as well as an onboard mechanic. It was used mainly for infantry support and often as just a land-based pillbox for island defence by 1944. This diminished their tactical effectiveness, and too few were built by the Japanese war machine to give this impressive design the impact it deserved.

SPECIFICATIONS

COUNTRY OF ORIGIN: Japan
CREW: 5
WEIGHT: (with pontoons) 11,301kg (24,862lb); (without pontoons) 9571kg (21,056lb)
DIMENSIONS: length (with pontoons) 7.42m (24ft 4in); length (without pontoons) 4.83m (15ft 10in); width 2.79m (9ft 2in); height 2.34m (7ft 8in)
RANGE: land radius 199.5km (125 miles); water radius 149.6km (93 miles)
ARMOUR: 6–12mm (0.23–0.47in)
ARMAMENT: 1 x 37mm (1.46in) anti-tank gun; 2 x 7.7mm (0.303in) machine gun
POWERPLANT: 1 x 6-cylinder air-cooled diesel engine developing 110hp (82kW)
PERFORMANCE: maximum land speed 37km/h (23mph); maximum water speed 9.65km/h (6mph); fording amphibious

DD Sherman

The Duplex Drive (DD) Sherman was born from a British concept, designed to allow tanks to float in water during amphibious operations. Development began in 1941, with a collapsible fabric screen and rubber air tubes being fitted to a boat-shaped platform welded onto a Sherman tank. The tank was powered in the water by two rear propellers. Once in shallow water, the screen could be collapsed and the tank was ready for conventional use. The vehicle was rather slow and could only be used in fairly calm waters. However, the Sherman's main gun proved very useful in supporting amphibious landings, in particular those on D-Day in June 1944, and the tank was a nasty surprise for the Germans, whose attempts to develop a similar concept had failed.

SPECIFICATIONS

COUNTRY OF ORIGIN: United States
CREW: 5
WEIGHT: 32,284kg (71,174lb)
DIMENSIONS: length 6.35m (20ft 10in); width 2.81m (9ft 3in); height 3.96m (13ft)
RANGE: 240km (149 miles)

ARMOUR: 12–51mm (0.47–2in)
ARMAMENT: one 75mm (2.95in) gun; two 7.62mm (0.3in) machine guns
POWERPLANT: one Ford GAA V-8 petrol engine developing 400 or 500hp (335.6 or 373kW)
PERFORMANCE: maximum water speed 4 knots; fording amphibious; vertical obstacle 0.61m (2ft); trench 2.26m (7ft 5in)

CGV 1906

The French automobile company of Charron, Giradot & Voigt (CGV) was, at the turn of the twentieth century, a producer of racing cars. However, with the growth in demand for military vehicles, CGV took a touring-car chassis and fitted it with an armoured barbette mounting an 8mm (0.31in) rear-facing machine gun. This vehicle was presented at the Paris Car Exhibition in 1902. Tests conducted on a new model in Russia in 1905 brought it up to production standard. Only about 12 CGV cars were produced between 1905 and 1908. Russia was a significant export market; indeed, in 1905, one of the vehicles was used to put down rioting in St Petersburg.

SPECIFICATIONS

COUNTRY OF ORIGIN: France
CREW: 4
WEIGHT: 3500kg (7700lb)
DIMENSIONS: length 4.46m (14ft 7in); width 1.85m (6ft 1in); height 2.47m (8ft 1in)
RANGE: 600km (373 miles)
ARMOUR: 6mm (0.23in)
ARMAMENT: 1 x 8mm (0.31in) MG
POWERPLANT: 1 x GCV 4-cylinder petrol, developing 30hp (22kW)
PERFORMANCE: maximum road speed: 45km/h (28mph)

Lanchester

Originally designed to support air bases and retrieve downed pilots, the Lanchester was the most numerous armoured car in service after the Rolls-Royce by the end of 1914. A year later they were formed into armoured car squadrons. The engine of the original car was retained, but the hull was much modified. The army took control of operations at the end of 1915 and decided to use the Rolls-Royce as the standard armoured car, Lanchesters being phased out of service. However, many were sent with navy crews to the Russians, with whom they served with some distinction in terrain as varied as Persia, Romania and Galicia. Reliable and fast, they spearheaded armoured columns and were used for reconnaissance before being shipped back to the United Kingdom.

SPECIFICATIONS

COUNTRY OF ORIGIN: United Kingdom
CREW: 4
WEIGHT: 4700kg (10,362lb)
DIMENSIONS: length 4.88m (16ft); width 1.93m (6ft 4in); height 2.28m (7ft 6in)
RANGE: 290km (180 miles)
ARMOUR: unknown
ARMAMENT: 1 x Vickers 7.7mm (0.303in) machine gun
POWERPLANT: 1 x 60hp (45kW) Lanchester petrol engine
PERFORMANCE: maximum speed 80km/h (50mph)

Pavesi 35 PS

The Pavesi 35 PS emerged from Italian inter-war experiments as an alternative to tracked armoured vehicles. It was developed by the agricultural vehicle company Pavesi-Tolotti of Milan, and consisted of a small armoured car driven by four outsize spoked wheels. Each wheel had a 1.55m (5ft 1in) diameter with broad metal rims for powerful cross-country movement. The clearance provided by the wheels was 0.75m (2ft 6in) and trenches of 1.4m (4ft 7in) width could be crossed. Armament was provided by a single machine gun mounted in the central rotating turret, and later experiments incorporated a 57mm (2.24in) cannon. In use until the late 1920s, it was manufactured in later years by the Fiat company.

SPECIFICATIONS

COUNTRY OF ORIGIN: Italy
CREW: 2
WEIGHT: 5000kg (11,023lb)
DIMENSIONS: length 4m (13ft 2in); width 2.18m (7ft 2in); height 2.2m (7ft 2in)
RANGE: not available
ARMOUR: not available
ARMAMENT: 1 x 8mm (0.31in) machine gun
POWERPLANT: 1 x Pavesi 4-cylinder petrol, developing 35hp (26kW)
PERFORMANCE: maximum road speed: 30km/h (19mph)

Austin-Putilov

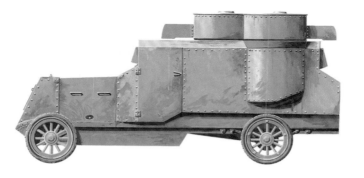

The Austin-Putilov was a British design, though it was mostly produced and used in Russia. The Russians took the basic chassis (all that could be supplied by the over-stretched British production lines) and modified it considerably to cope with the harsh Russian conditions, including later replacing the rear wheels with tracks and adding additional armour and rear steering. Both in terms of numbers and performance, the Austin-Putilov was the most important armoured car the Russians possessed during World War I. Many also saw action in the internal fighting surrounding the October revolution and afterwards in the Russian Civil War. After 1918, some saw service with the Polish Army, with a number being sold to Japan. It was an extremely rugged vehicle.

SPECIFICATIONS

COUNTRY OF ORIGIN: United Kingdom/Russia
CREW: 5
WEIGHT: 5200kg (11,440lb)
DIMENSIONS: length 4.88m (16ft); width 1.95m (6ft 4.75in); height 2.40m (7ft 10.5in)
RANGE: 200km (124 miles)
ARMOUR: 8mm (0.32in)
ARMAMENT: 2 x Maxim machine guns
POWERPLANT: 1 x 50hp (37.3kW) Austin petrol engine
PERFORMANCE: maximum speed 50km/h (31mph)

Autoblindé Peugeot

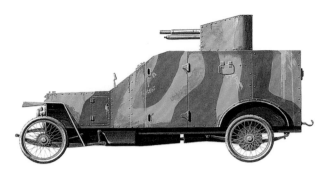

The Autoblindé Peugeot entered service in World War I as one of the first generation of armoured cars. Armoured cars is literally what they were – French commercial road cars covered with armoured panels. Two such vehicles emerged in late 1914. These were the AM Renault 20CV and the AC Peugeot 18CV. The Renault vehicle was armed with a 7.62mm (0.3in) machine gun, while the Peugeot received a 37mm (1.46in) cannon, but the design of the cars was so similar that both armament and armour were interchangeable. About 150 Peugeots were produced during World War I. Post-war service included combat with the French Army in Africa, and service with the Polish Army in the 1920s against Russia.

SPECIFICATIONS

COUNTRY OF ORIGIN: France
CREW: 4 or 5
WEIGHT: 4900kg (10,800lb)
DIMENSIONS: length 4.8m (15ft 9in); width 1.8m (5ft 10in); height 2.8m (9ft 2in)
RANGE: 140km (85 miles)
ARMOUR: 5.5mm (0.22in)
ARMAMENT: 1 x 37mm (1.46in) cannon or 1 x 7.62mm (0.3in) MG
POWERPLANT: Peugeot 146 4-cylinder petrol, developing 45hp (34kW)
PERFORMANCE: maximum road speed: 40km/h (25mph)

Daimler/15

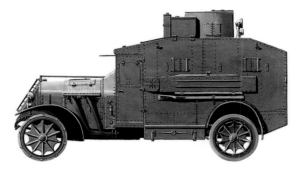

In late 1914, the companies Daimler, Büssing and Ehrhardt were commissioned to develop a prototype armoured car for Germany. Because of other production commitments, Daimler was not able to field its prototype until December 1915, but, following testing, prototype models of the Daimler/15 went on to serve on all fronts with reasonable success. The Daimler/15 consisted of an all-wheel-drive car chassis with an armoured structure of Krupp riveted chromium-nickel stainless steel plates. Dual tyres at the rear and sand rims on the front wheels prevented the vehicle sinking into soft ground. Armament was provided by three machine guns. In many ways the Daimler/15's carrying capacity of 10 men made it an incipient APC.

SPECIFICATIONS

COUNTRY OF ORIGIN: Germany
CREW: 10
WEIGHT: 9800kg (21,605lb)
DIMENSIONS: length 5.61m (18ft 4in); width 2.03m (6ft 7in); height 3.85m (12ft 7in)
RANGE: 250km (155 miles)
ARMOUR: not known
ARMAMENT: 3 x 7.92mm (0.31in) MG
POWERPLANT: 1 x Daimler Model 4-cylinder petrol, developing 80hp (60kW)
PERFORMANCE: maximum road speed: 38km/h (24mph)

Rolls-Royce

In 1914, the Royal Naval Air Service noted how the Belgians were using armoured cars to carry out raids on the advancing German Army. They decided to convert some of the Rolls-Royce Silver Ghost cars in their possession. The conversion was a success, and the Admiralty gave permission for an official armoured car based on the Silver Ghost chassis. With strengthened suspension and added armour, the Rolls-Royce saw service all over the world from March 1915, notably in Africa and the Arabian peninsula, where they proved to have excellent cross-country mobility. They were most at home in terrain where they could roam far and wide. They continued in service until being replaced in British Army service in 1922, although some were used in India well into World War II.

SPECIFICATIONS

COUNTRY OF ORIGIN: United Kingdom
CREW: 3 or 4
WEIGHT: 3400kg (7495lb)
DIMENSIONS: length 5.03m (16ft 6in); width 1.91m (6ft 3in); height 2.55m (8ft 5in)
RANGE: 240km (150 miles)
ARMOUR: 9mm (0.35in)
ARMAMENT: Vickers 7.7mm (0.303in) machine gun
POWERPLANT: 1 x 40/50hp (30/37kW) Rolls-Royce petrol engine
PERFORMANCE: maximum road speed 95km/h (60mph)

Büssing A5P

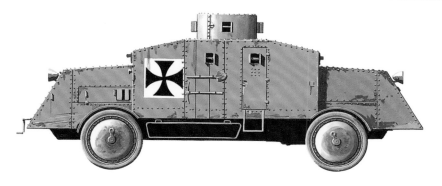

The Büssing company originally specialized in heavy farm vehicles, which then became models for several German military machines. The firm received its first orders for military vehicles in 1910, producing artillery tractors and supply trailers. In November 1914, Büssing, Daimler and Ehrhardt were requested to develop an armoured car with all-wheel drive. Two years later, Büssing's A5P was began production. It was powered by one of Büssing's legendary 6-cylinder truck engines, and featured a large steel armoured body. Inside the vehicle were 10 crew, six of them working three machine guns. Some A5Ps received two 20mm (0.79in) cannon. The A5P served in Romania and Russia until the end of 1917.

SPECIFICATIONS

COUNTRY OF ORIGIN: Germany
CREW: 10
WEIGHT: 10,250kg (22,600lb)
DIMENSIONS: length 9.5m (31ft 2in); width 2.1m (6ft 10in); height not available
RANGE: 250km (155 miles)
ARMOUR: not available
ARMAMENT: 3 x 7.92mm (0.31in) MG
POWERPLANT: 1 x Büssing petrol, developing 90hp (67kW)
PERFORMANCE: maximum road speed: 35km/h (21mph)

Lancia Autoblinda IZ

The Autoblinda IZ was an early foray into armoured-car manufacturing by the Lancia company of Italy. It was based on the chassis of the Lancia IZ light truck but armoured with 6mm (0.24in) steel plates. Originally it had a double-turret construction with three 7.92mm (0.31in) Maxim or 8mm (0.31mm) St Etienne machine guns. The small cupola mounting a single gun at the top was later removed and the gun located in a ball mounting at the rear of the vehicle. In 1915, the first production year, 20 such vehicles were built. Subsequently, the IZ served throughout World War I, and in World War II could still be found in Italian East Africa and Libya.

SPECIFICATIONS

COUNTRY OF ORIGIN: Italy
CREW: 6 or 7
WEIGHT: 3700kg (8157lb)
DIMENSIONS: length 5.4m (17ft 8in); width 1.82m (5ft 11in); height 2.4m (7ft 10in)
RANGE: 300km (186 miles)
ARMOUR: steel 6mm (0.24in)
ARMAMENT: 3 x 7.92mm (0.31in) Maxim or 8mm (0.31in) St Etienne machine guns
POWERPLANT: 1 x Lancia 4-cylinder petrol, developing 70hp (52kW) at 2200rpm
PERFORMANCE: maximum road speed: 60km/h (37mph)

Laffly-White Auto-Mitrailleuse

The Laffly-White Auto-Mitrailleuse ('machine-gun car') was created by combining an armoured body designed by the French company Laffly with the truck chassis from the US company White. White trucks were imported into France from 1915 and, in 1918, Laffly began production of its armoured car. In spite of cumbersome dimensions, the Laffly-White served into World War II after active use in the Levant and North Africa in colonial police roles. By 1939, its reliability and durability had made it popular, but its slow speed, largely ineffective 37mm (1.46in) gun and high profile rendered it obsolete against German vehicle technology. By 1940, most were replaced by new Panhard vehicles.

SPECIFICATIONS

COUNTRY OF ORIGIN: France
CREW: 4
WEIGHT: 6000kg (13,228lb)
DIMENSIONS: length: 5.6m (18ft 4in); width: 2.1m (6ft 10in); height: 2.75m (9ft)
RANGE: 250km (155 miles)
ARMOUR: 8mm (0.31in)
ARMAMENT: 1 x 37mm (1.46in) cannon; 2 x 8mm (0.31in) MGs
POWERPLANT: 1 x White 4-cylinder petrol, developing 35hp (26kW)
PERFORMANCE: maximum road speed: 45km/h (28mph)

Daimler DZVR 1919

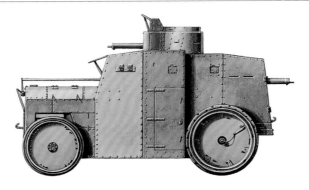

The Daimler DZVR was one of several German vehicles created after the end of World War I under the terms of the Treaty of Versailles. Interwar Germany required security vehicles to police internal civil unrest and problems on its eastern borders, and 38 DZVR vehicles were ordered for this purpose. The DZVR was based on the chassis of the KD1 artillery tractor, and 1000 of these vehicles were left over from the war. Armour plate, 12mm (0.47in) thick, encased the six-man crew compartment, and a revolving turret at the top held a searchlight. During the 1920s, the searchlight was replaced by a Maxim machine gun. The DZVR remained in police use until the early 1940s.

SPECIFICATIONS

COUNTRY OF ORIGIN: Germany
CREW: 6
WEIGHT: 10,500kg (23,149lb)
DIMENSIONS: length 5.9m (19ft 4in); width 2.1m (6ft 10in); height 3.1m (10ft 2in)
RANGE: 150km (93 miles)
ARMOUR: (steel) 12mm (0.47in)
ARMAMENT: 2 x 7.92mm (0.31in) Maxim MGs
POWERPLANT: 1 x Daimler M1574 4-cylinder petrol, developing 100hp (75kW)
PERFORMANCE: maximum road speed: 43km/h (27mph)

Schupo-Sonderwagen 21

Though the Treaty of Versailles (1919) did not permit the Weimar Republic to equip itself with armoured units, the Allied victors did permit the construction of 150 armoured cars for German police service. Consequently, between 1921 and 1925, three companies – Daimler, Ehrhardt and Benz – were engaged in the production of the Schupo-Sonderwagen 21. The Schupo was a huge vehicle weighing in at 11,000kg (24,250lb). Its extreme weight was caused by large amounts of chromium-nickel plated armour, steel-shod wheels, three Maxim 08 machine guns, and nine crew. The front end of the vehicle was designed to batter its way through street barricades. Around 100 Schupo vehicles were produced.

SPECIFICATIONS

COUNTRY OF ORIGIN: Germany
CREW: 9
WEIGHT: 11,000kg (24,250lb)
DIMENSIONS: length 6.5m (21ft 4in); width 2.41m (7ft 11in); height 3.45m (11ft 4in)
RANGE: 350km (218 miles)
ARMOUR: chromium-nickel plated
ARMAMENT: 3 x 7.92mm (0.31in) Maxim 08 MGs
POWERPLANT: 1 x Ehrhardt 4-cylinder petrol, developing 80hp (60kW)
PERFORMANCE: maximum road speed: 56km/h (35mph)

BA-10

The BA-10 was built on the chassis of the GAZ-AAA commercial truck (which was modified and reinforced to cope with the extra weight) and first appeared in 1932. It was a bulky, functional piece of equipment whose World War I ancestry was evident from its outmoded appearance. Despite its weight, the BA-10 proved well-suited to the terrain and distances of the Soviet Union, and its main armament was as good as many tanks. The Germans captured large numbers of the vehicle after the invasion of Russian in June 1941 and used them for anti-partisan duties both in the USSR and in the Balkans, a role in which it excelled. Those that remained in Soviet hands were replaced in frontline service after 1942 and stripped down, to be used as armoured personnel carriers.

SPECIFICATIONS

COUNTRY OF ORIGIN: Soviet Union
CREW: 4
WEIGHT: 7500kg (16,500lb)
DIMENSIONS: length 4.70m (15ft 5in); width 2.09m (6ft 10.5in); height 2.42m (7ft 11.25in)
RANGE: 320km (199 miles)
ARMOUR: up to 25mm (0.98in)
ARMAMENT: 1 x 37mm (1.46in)/45mm (1.77in) gun; one 7.62mm (0.3in) machine gun
POWERPLANT: 1 x GAZ-M 14-cylinder water-cooled petrol engine developing 85hp (63kW)
PERFORMANCE: maximum speed 87km/h (54mph); fording 0.6m (1ft 11in); vertical obstacle 0.38m (1ft 3in); 0.5m (1ft 7in)

BA-20

The BA-20 was a Russian scout/ command vehicle, which replaced the FAI-M light armoured car. Its truck ancestry is visually clear, and it used the chassis of the GAZ-M1 truck with a superstructure of armoured steel plate. This plate had a thickness of 4–6mm (0.16–0.24in); thick enough to protect against small-arms fire. The BA-20 had a small turret with a 7.62mm (0.3in) DT machine gun and slightly sloping armoured plates to enhance missile deflection. Two basic versions were produced: the BA-20 with a clothes-line aerial and the later BA-20M which had a whip aerial. A major upgrade in 1939 using the 6 x 4 GAZ-21 truck chassis was abandoned before production began.

SPECIFICATIONS

COUNTRY OF ORIGIN: Soviet Union
CREW: 2
WEIGHT: 2340kg (5160lb)
DIMENSIONS: length 4.1m (13ft 5in); width 1.8m (5ft 10in); height 2.3m (7ft 6in)
RANGE: 350km (220 miles)
ARMOUR: (steel) 4–6mm (0.16–0.24in)
ARMAMENT: 1 x 7.62mm (0.3in) MG
POWERPLANT: 1 x GAZ-M1 4-cylinder petrol, developing 50hp (37kW)
PERFORMANCE: maximum road speed: 90km/h (56mph)

BA-64

With the onset of the German–Soviet war in 1941, the Red Army discovered that most of its armoured cars were inadequately armoured and outclassed by German vehicles. The BA-64 was an attempt to remedy these problems. Its armoured plates were angled steeply to increase bullet and missile deflection, the suspension was strengthened over previous vehicles to improve off-road durability and it had bullet-proof tyres and bullet-proof glass in the driver's observation visor. Most significantly, it had four-wheel drive which enabled it to climb 30-degree slopes. Armament remained light; a single 7.62mm (0.3in) Degtyarev machine gun was mounted in the turret.

SPECIFICATIONS

COUNTRY OF ORIGIN: Soviet Union
CREW: 2
WEIGHT: 2360kg (5200lb)
DIMENSIONS: length 3.67m (12 ft 0.5in); width 1.52m (4ft 11in); height 1.88m (6ft 2in)
RANGE: 560km (350 miles)
ARMOUR: (steel) 4–15mm (0.16–0.59in)
ARMAMENT: 1 x 7.62mm (0.3in) MG
POWERPLANT: 1 x GAZ-MM 4-cylinder petrol, developing 54hp (40kW)
PERFORMANCE: maximum road speed: 80km/h (50mph)

SdKfz 231

Although the SdKfz 231 was originally developed at the Kazan test centre in the Soviet Union, the vehicle was a German design intended for German use. A 6 x 4 Daimler-Benz truck chassis was used as the basis, and an armoured hull and turret added. Production ran from 1932–35, by which time around 1000 had been built. The hull was too heavy for the chassis, though, which resulted in poor cross-country performance. However, they were used on roads to good effect during the occupation of Czechoslovakia and the campaigns in Poland and France in 1939–40, their appearance alone having a good propaganda value. Their greatest achievement was to provide an invaluable training vehicle for the German Army's development during the 1930s.

SPECIFICATIONS

COUNTRY OF ORIGIN: Germany
CREW: 4
WEIGHT: 5700kg (12,566lb)
DIMENSIONS: length (overall) 5.57m (18ft 3in); width 1.82m (5ft 11in); height 2.25m (7ft 5in)
RANGE: 250km (155 miles)
ARMOUR: 8mm (0.31in)
ARMAMENT: 1 x 20mm (0.79in) KwK 38 cannon; 1 x coaxial 7.62mm (0.3in) machine gun
POWERPLANT: 1 x Daimler-Benz, Bussing-NAG or Magirus water-cooled petrol engine developing between 60 and 80hp (45 and 60kW)
PERFORMANCE: maximum road speed 65km/h (40mph); fording 0.6m (1ft 11in)

Sumida M.2593

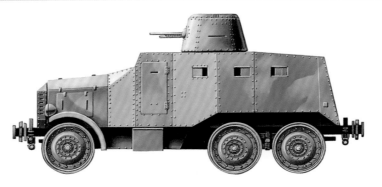

One of the most ingenious armoured vehicles of the interwar period was the Japanese Sumida M.2593. Produced from 1933 by the Ishikawajima Motor Works, it had the option of travelling by either road or rail. Solid road wheels could be exchanged for railway wheels carried on the side of the vehicle, the front and rear wheels adaptable to different rail gauges. After the swap it could drive at 60km/h (37mph) on rails, powered by its four-cylinder petrol engine. The Sumida proved useful in covering the great distances of mainland China during the Japanese invasion of the late 1930s, but its solid wheels made it unsuitable for off-road manoeuvre.

SPECIFICATIONS

COUNTRY OF ORIGIN: Japan
CREW: 6
WEIGHT: 7000kg (15,432lb)
DIMENSIONS: length 6.57m (21ft 7in); width 1.9m (6ft 3in); height 2.95m (9ft 8in)
RANGE: 240km (150 miles)
ARMOUR: 10mm (0.39in)
ARMAMENT: 1 x MG
POWERPLANT: 1 x 4-cylinder petrol, developing 45hp (34kW)
PERFORMANCE: maximum road speed: 40km/h (25mph); maximum rail speed: 60km/h (37mph)

WZ/34

Prior to 1933, Poland's armoured car was the WZ/28, an unsatisfactory halftrack design using the chassis of the French Citroën-Kegresse B2 10CV. Ninety such vehicles were made, but, by 1938, 87 of them had been converted into a wheeled 4 x 2 configuration and renamed the WZ/34. The WZ/-34 shape had a recognizable car heritage, though the rear of the vehicle was built up into a high turret mounting either a 37mm (1.46in) SA-18 Puteaux L/21 gun or a 7.92mm (0.31in) Hotchkiss wz.25 machine gun. Neither the armament nor the meagre 6mm (0.23in) riveted armour plate provided any realistic defence against German panzers during the Polish invasion in September 1939.

SPECIFICATIONS

COUNTRY OF ORIGIN: Poland
CREW: 2
WEIGHT: 2200kg (4850lb)
DIMENSIONS: length 3.62m (11ft 10in); width 1.91m (6ft 3in); height 2.21m (7ft 3in)
RANGE: 250km (155 miles)
ARMOUR: 6mm (0.24in)
ARMAMENT: 1 x 37mm (1.46in) SA-18 Puteaux L/21 gun; or 1 x 7.92mm (0.31in) Hotchkiss wz.25 machine gun
POWERPLANT: 1 x Citroën B-T4 6-cylinder petrol, developing 20hp (15kW); or 1 x Fiat 6-cylinder petrol developing 25hp (19kW)
PERFORMANCE: maximum road speed: 40km/h (25mph)

SdKfz 222

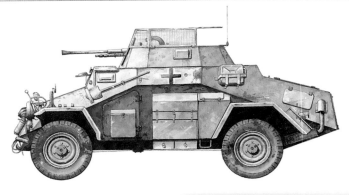

When the Nazis began to rearm the German Army in the mid-1930s, a request was made for a series of light armoured cars based on a standard chassis. The demanding requirements could not be met by adapting commercial models, so a new design was produced. The first production SdKfz 222 appeared in 1938, and thereafter became the standard armoured reconnaissance car of the Wehrmacht. A reliable and popular vehicle, the SdKfz 222 served the army well during the Blitzkrieg against Poland and France in 1939–40, and later in North Africa. However, its restricted range, made evident in the latter theatre, proved problematic during the invasion of the Soviet Union in 1941. That said, it remained in German service in western Europe until the end of World War II.

SPECIFICATIONS

COUNTRY OF ORIGIN: Germany
CREW: 3
WEIGHT: 4800kg (10,582lb)
DIMENSIONS: length 4.80m (14ft 9in); width 1.95m (6ft 5in); height 2m (6ft 7in) with grenade screen
RANGE: 300km (186 miles)
ARMOUR: 14.5–30mm (0.6–1.2in)
ARMAMENT: 1 x 20mm (0.79in) KwK 30 cannon; 1 x 7.92 (0.31in) MG34 machine gun
POWERPLANT: 1 x Horch/Auto-Union V8-108 water-cooled petrol engine developing 81hp (60kW)
PERFORMANCE: maximum road speed 80km/h (50mph); fording 0.6m (1ft 11in)

Landsverk 180

The Landsverk 180 armoured car was produced from 1938. Its foundation was the chassis of a Scania-Vabis truck with 6x4 wheel drive, though the Landsverk 180 had twin wheels on the rear axles, 10 wheels in total. Armour plate was riveted to the chassis, creating a boxy car-like shape capped by a small turret mounting a Madsen 20mm (0.78in) cannon and coaxial 7.92mm (0.31in) machine gun. Other machine guns were located just beneath the turret and facing backwards out of the rear of the hull. A powerful Scania-Vabis engine gave the Landsverk 180 a respectable top road speed of 80km/h (50mph), but the vehicle was soon obsolete in the context of modern World War II armour.

SPECIFICATIONS

COUNTRY OF ORIGIN: Sweden
CREW: 5
WEIGHT: 7000kg (15,432lb)
DIMENSIONS: length 5.87m (19ft 3in); width 2.5m (8ft 2in); height 2.33m (7ft 7in)
RANGE: 290km (180 miles)
ARMOUR: 8.5mm (0.33in)
ARMAMENT: 1 x 37mm (1.46in) cannon; 3 x 7.92mm (0.31in) MG
POWERPLANT: 1 x Scania-Vabis 6-cylinder diesel, developing 80hp (60kW)
PERFORMANCE: maximum road speed: 80km/h (50mph)

SdKfz 232 (8 Rad)

The SdKfz 232 (8 Rad) was essentially the same as the SdKfz 231 (8 Rad), except that it was fitted with a long-range aerial antenna over the top of the turret. A 6 x 4 SdKfz 231 was produced between 1932 and 1935, but this had limited off-road performance. The SdKfz 232 (8 Rad) solved this problem admirably with its 8 x 8 configuration; they could even travel through the infamous autumnal muds of the eastern front and the sands of North Africa without impediment. Yet they were very expensive and complicated to produce, and fewer than 1500 were manufactured. Both the SdKfz 231 and 232 have the suffix 8 Rad (8-wheel) to distinguish them from their six-wheel counterparts.

SPECIFICATIONS

COUNTRY OF ORIGIN: Germany
CREW: 4
WEIGHT: 9100kg (20,062lb)
DIMENSIONS: length 5.58m (18ft 4in); width 2.2m (7ft 2in); height 2.9m (9ft 6in)
RANGE: 300km (186 miles)
ARMOUR: 15–30mm (0.59–1.18in)
ARMAMENT: 1 x 20mm (0.79in) cannon; 1 x 7.92mm (0.31in) MG
POWERPLANT: 1 x Büssing-NAG L8V-Gs petrol, developing 160hp (119kW) at 3000rpm
PERFORMANCE: maximum road speed: 85km/h (53mph); fording: 1m (3ft 3in); gradient: 30 percent; vertical obstacle: 0.5m (1ft 8in); trench: 1.25m (4ft 1in) (4.1ft)

Panhard et Levassor Type 178

The Panhard 178 was designed in the mid-1930s as a 4x4 armoured reconnaissance vehicle for the French Army. Its most common armament was a single 25mm (0.98in) cannon or two 7.5mm (0.29in) machine guns. French production of the Panhard 178 ended with the German occupation in 1940. The Germans, however, were impressed with the design and used large numbers under the designation Panzerspähwagen P 204(f). Some of these were turned into anti-aircraft platforms by fitting them with 37mm (1.46in) anti-aircraft guns. French production of the 178 recommenced in August 1944 after the liberation of Paris, though with a larger turret and 47mm (1.85in) gun. These endured in French Army service until 1960.

SPECIFICATIONS

COUNTRY OF ORIGIN: France
CREW: 4
WEIGHT: 8300kg (18,300lb)
DIMENSIONS: Length: 4.8m (15.74ft); width: 2.01m (6.59ft); height: 2.33m (7.64ft)
RANGE: 300km (190 miles)
ARMOUR: 18mm (0.7in)
ARMAMENT: 1 x 25mm (0.98in) cannon; 1 x 7.5mm (0.29in) MG
POWERPLANT: 1 x Renault 4-cylinder petrol, developing 180hp (134kW)
PERFORMANCE: Maximum road speed: 72km/h (45mph); fording: 0.6m (2ft); gradient: 40 percent; vertical obstacle: 0.3m (1ft); trench: 0.6m (2ft)

Daimler Scout Car

When the British Army was forming its first armoured divisions in the late 1930s, a requirement was issued for a 4 x 4 scout car for reconnaissance purposes. The Daimler Scout Car was the result. Entering production just prior to the start of World War II, it was still being made at the end of the war and was to prove one of the most successful reconnaissance vehicles in use by any army during the war. Its inconspicuous nature and excellent mobility compensated for lack of armour and armament, deficiencies not necessarily fatal to vehicles that move fast on the battlefield and do not stand and engage in firefights with enemy armour. The folding roof was removed on later models, as experience showed it was rarely used operationally and gave minimal cover in any case.

SPECIFICATIONS

COUNTRY OF ORIGIN: United Kingdom
CREW: 2
WEIGHT: 3000kg (6614lb)
DIMENSIONS: length 3.23m (10ft 7in); width 1.72m (5ft 8in); height 1.50m (4ft 11in)
RANGE: 322km (200 miles)
ARMOUR: 14.5–30mm (0.6–1.2in)
ARMAMENT: 1 x 7.7mm (0.303in) Bren machine gun
POWERPLANT: 1 x Daimler 6-cylinder petrol engine developing 55hp (41kW)
PERFORMANCE: maximum speed 88.5km/h (55mph); fording 0.6m (1ft 11in); vertical obstacle 0.53m (1ft 9in); trench 1.22m (4ft)

M39 Pantserwagen

The M39 was produced by the DAF company in the build-up to World War II, resisting Dutch Army requests to license-build British armoured cars. It was a well-made 6 x 4 armoured car with an all-welded hull, a rear-mounted Ford Mercury V8 engine and a well-sloped glacis plate. A useful set of driving controls at the rear of the vehicle allowed the rear machine-gunner to control the vehicle in reverse in an emergency. At the front of the hull, two small wheels prevented the forward edge of the glacis plate digging into the ground on rough terrain. After the fall of the Netherlands in 1940, M39s were pressed into German service as Pz. SpWg L202h.

SPECIFICATIONS

COUNTRY OF ORIGIN: Netherlands
CREW: 5
WEIGHT: 6000kg (13,228lb)
DIMENSIONS: length 4.75m (15ft 7in); width 2.03m (6ft 7in); height 2.16m (7ft 1in)
RANGE: 320km (199 miles)
ARMOUR: 12mm (0.47in)
ARMAMENT: 1 x 37mm (1.46in) cannon; 3 x 8mm (0.31in) MGs
POWERPLANT: 1 x Ford Mercury V-8 petrol, developing 95hp (71kW)
PERFORMANCE: maximum road speed: 60km/h (37mph)

Marmon Herrington

In 1938, the South African government ordered the development of an armoured car, based on foreign components but to be assembled in South Africa. The chassis and engine were made by Ford, the transmission by Marmon Herrington in the US and the armament was imported from the UK. At the time it was first produced, the Marmon Herrington was the only armoured car available to British and South African forces in any numbers, and it saw extensive service in the Western Desert in the campaign against Rommel's Afrika Korps. Well-liked and sturdy, the vehicle was surprisingly effective despite light armour and armament, being relatively easy to maintain under operational conditions. The vehicles were much modified to suit local conditions, and were fitted in the field with many different weapons.

SPECIFICATIONS
COUNTRY OF ORIGIN: South Africa
CREW: 4
WEIGHT: 6000kg (13,227lb)
DIMENSIONS: length 4.88m (16ft); width 1.93m (6ft 4in); height 2.28m (7ft 6in)
RANGE: 322km (200 miles)
ARMOUR: 12mm (0.47in)
ARMAMENT: 1 x Vickers 7.7mm (0.303in) machine gun; 1 x Boys 13.97mm (0.55in) anti-tank rifle; 1 x 7.7mm (0.303in) Bren Gun
POWERPLANT: 1 x Ford V-8 petrol engine
PERFORMANCE: maximum speed 80.5km/h (50mph)

SdKfz 234

The SdKfz 234 was produced by
Büssing-NAG in response to a 1940
German Army requirement for an 8 x
8 armoured car suitable for operations
in hot climates. More streamlined than
the earlier 231 series and with thicker
armour, the 234's excellent performance
ensured its place as probably the best
vehicle of its type to see service in World
War II with any army. The most famous
model was the 234/2 Puma, which used
the turret intended for the Leopard light
tank. This gave sufficient firepower to deal
with most enemy reconnaissance armour
encountered. The quality of the vehicle
may be judged by the fact that, despite
its high cost of manufacture, the vehicle
was the only reconnaissance vehicle kept
in production by the starved German war
industry in 1945.

SPECIFICATIONS

COUNTRY OF ORIGIN: Germany
CREW: 4
WEIGHT: 11,740kg (25,882lb)
DIMENSIONS: length 6.80m (22ft 4in); width 2.33m
(7ft 7in); height 2.38m (7ft 10in)
RANGE: 1000km (621 miles)
ARMOUR: 5–15mm (0.19–0.59in)
ARMAMENT: 1 x 20mm (0.79in) KwK 30/50mm KwK
39/1 cannon; 1 x coaxial 7.92mm (0.31in)
machine gun
POWERPLANT: 1 x Tatra Model 103 diesel engine
developing 210hp (157kW)
PERFORMANCE: maximum road speed 85km/h
(53mph); fording 1.2m (3ft 11in); vertical obstacle
0.5m (1ft 8in); trench 1.35m (4ft 5in)

Autoblinda 41

The Autoblinda had its origins in a dual requirement by the Italians for use as an armoured car for the cavalry divisions and a high-performance car for use in policing Italy's numerous African colonies. The Autoblinda 40 was produced to meet both these needs. The Autoblinda 41 was fitted with the turret of the L6/40 light tank, complete with its 20mm (0.79in) cannon. This was a more effective combination, therefore production centred on this version. The vehicle could be adapted for desert use, with special sand tyres, and could also be adapted to run on railway tracks, being extensively used in this capacity for anti-partisan duties in the Balkans. One of the most numerous Italian armoured cars of World War II, the vehicle also saw action in the Western Desert and Tunisia.

SPECIFICATIONS

COUNTRY OF ORIGIN: Italy
CREW: 4
WEIGHT: 7500kg (16,500lb)
DIMENSIONS: length 5.20m (17ft 1.5in); width 1.92m (6ft 4.5in); height 2.48m (7ft 11.5in)
RANGE: 400km (248 miles)

ARMOUR: 6–40mm (0.23–1.57in)
ARMAMENT: one 20mm (0.79in) Breda cannon; two 8mm (0.32in) machine guns
POWERPLANT: 1 x SAP Abm 1 6-cylinder water-cooled inline petrol engine developing 80hp (60kW)
PERFORMANCE: maximum road speed 78km/h (49mph); fording 0.7m (2ft 3in); vertical obstacle 0.3m (12in); trench 0.4m (1ft 4in)

Daimler Mk I

The Daimler armoured car was based on the same design as the Daimler scout car. Outwardly similar, it weighed almost twice as much and had a two-man turret. Work began in August 1939, but initial problems meant that the first production vehicles did not appear until April 1941. A total of 2694 were built. The turret was the same as that designed for the Tetrarch light airborne tank. The vehicle was equipped with hydraulic disc brakes, one of the earliest vehicles to be fitted with the system. First employed in North Africa, the vehicle established itself as an excellent addition to reconnaissance units, despite its limited combat capability, giving good all-round performance and reliability. The Daimler continued to serve for many years after the end of World War II.

SPECIFICATIONS

COUNTRY OF ORIGIN: United Kingdom
CREW: 3
WEIGHT: 7500kg (16,535lb)
DIMENSIONS: length 3.96m (1ft 11in); width 2.44m (8ft); height 2.24m (7ft 4in)
RANGE: 330km (205 miles)
ARMOUR: 14.5–30mm (0.6–1.2in)
ARMAMENT: 1 x 2-pounder gun; one Besa 7.92mm (0.31in) coaxial machine gun
POWERPLANT: 1 x Daimler 6-cylinder petrol engine developing 95hp (71kW)
PERFORMANCE: maximum speed 80.5km/h (50mph); fording 0.6m (1ft 11in); vertical obstacle 0.53m (1ft 9in); trench 1.22m (4ft)

TANKS AND ARMOURED VEHICLES 1900–1945 ARMOURED VEHICLES

Humber Mk I

Numerically, the Humber was the most important British armoured car of World War II, a total of 5400 being produced. Based on a pre-war wheeled light tank design by Guy, the Humber was initially fitted only with machine guns, which meant it was outgunned by the opposition. It was later upgunned and was used in North Africa from 1941 onwards, and wherever British troops were in action thereafter. Variants included a special radio carrier, known as Rear Link vehicle, which was fitted with a dummy gun, and an anti-aircraft version fitted with a special machine-gun mounting. The vehicle gave excellent service, and was still being used by some armies in the Far East in the early 1960s. Like most British-produced armoured vehicles, the Humber was rugged, reliable and operationally sound.

SPECIFICATIONS

COUNTRY OF ORIGIN: United Kingdom
CREW: 3 (4 in Mk III)
WEIGHT: 6850kg (15,102lb)
DIMENSIONS: length 4.57m (14ft 11in); width 2.18m (7ft 2in); height 2.34m (7ft 10in)
RANGE: 402km (250 miles)
ARMOUR: 14.5–30mm (0.6–1.2in)
ARMAMENT: 1 x 15mm (0.59in) gun; 1 x 7.92mm (0.31in) Besa machine gun
POWERPLANT: 1 x Rootes six-cylinder water-cooled petrol engine developing 90hp (77kW)
PERFORMANCE: maximum speed 72km/h (45mph); fording 0.6m (1ft 11in); vertical obstacle 0.533m (1ft 9in); trench 1.22m (4ft)

Churchill AVRE

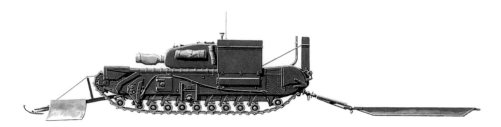

The Churchill Assault Vehicle Royal Engineers (AVRE) was borne out of the failure of the 1942 Dieppe raid where engineers were prevented from clearing obstacles by enemy fire. The tank was developed to transport engineers to the required spot and give protection, as well as carrying a heavy demolition weapon (special fittings were placed on the sides at the front for attaching devices). With a stripped interior to give extra storage space and a mortar capable of firing a heavy demolition charge, they performed excellently during their first action, clearing the way for the Normandy landings on D-Day (6 June 1944). They remained in service with the British Army until the 1960s but the concept was so successful that AVREs are still used, the current model being the Centurion AVRE.

SPECIFICATIONS

COUNTRY OF ORIGIN: United Kingdom
CREW: 6
WEIGHT: 38,000kg (83,775lb)
DIMENSIONS: length 7.67m (25ft 2in); width 3.25m (10ft 8in); height 2.79m (9ft 2in)
RANGE: 193km (120 miles)

ARMOUR: 16–102mm (0.6–4in)
ARMAMENT: 1 x Petard 290mm (11.42in) spigot mortar; one 7.92mm (0.31in) Besa machine-gun
POWERPLANT: 1 x Bedford Twin-Six petrol engine developing 350hp (261kW)
PERFORMANCE: maximum road speed 24.9km/h (15.5mph); fording 1.02m (3ft 4in); vertical obstacle 0.76m (2ft 6in); trench 3.05m (10ft)

Churchill AVRE with Log Carpet

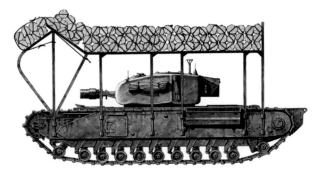

A similar arrangement was developed using linked logs. The roadway was laid under the front tracks and was pulled from its carrying frame as the AVRE moved forward. Like the Bobbin Carpet, the Log Carpet was intended to be a temporary measure only. After World War II, flexible metal roadways were developed to replace these earlier devices. The log carpet itself consisted of 100 152mm (6in) diameter logs, each 4.26m (14ft) long, bound together with wire rope. A removable steel frame was fitted above the AVRE superstructure carrying the looped mat, which was released over the front of the vehicle by detonating a light charge. The vehicle was one of a number developed for laying tracks over marshy ground or barbed wire for wheeled vehicles and infantry.

SPECIFICATIONS

COUNTRY OF ORIGIN: United Kingdom
CREW: 5
WEIGHT: 40,727kg (89,600lb)
DIMENSIONS: length 7.44m (24ft 5in); width 2.44m (8ft); height 3.45m (11ft 4in) (log carpet mounted above tank)
RANGE: 144.8km (90 miles)
ARMOUR: 16–102mm (0.6–4in)
ARMAMENT: 1 x Petard 290mm (11.42in) spigot mortar; one 7.92mm (0.31in) Besa machine gun
POWERPLANT: 1 x Bedford twin-six petrol engine developing 350hp (261kW)
PERFORMANCE: maximum road speed 20km/h (12.5mph); maximum cross-country speed about 12.8km/h (8mph); fording 1.02m (3ft 4in); vertical obstacle 0.76m (2ft 6in); trench 3.05m (10ft)

Churchill AVRE Fascine & Mat-Layer

The fascine-layer was developed from a technique used in ancient times and resurrected during World War I to allow tanks and other vehicles to cross ditches or soft ground, generally using bundles of brushwood to fill gaps or mats made of bundles of chespaling or hessian, linked up and laid out behind the tank using a roller mechanism. The tank was a standard Churchill AVRE with the devices attached to the front. The Bobbin Carpet used a hessian mat to cover wire obstacles and allow troops forward to assault the defences. The bobbins were carried well above the ground. When required the weighted free end of the carpet was dropped to the ground, the bobbin automatically unwinding itself as the tank rolled forward. This was first used during the 1942 Dieppe raid.

SPECIFICATIONS

COUNTRY OF ORIGIN: United Kingdom
CREW: 5
WEIGHT: 42,000kg (92,400lb)
DIMENSIONS: length 7.44m (24ft 5in); width 2.44m (8ft); height 5.49m (18ft)
RANGE: 130km (81 miles)

ARMOUR: 16–102mm (0.6–4in)
ARMAMENT: 1 x Petard 290mm (11.42in) spigot mortar; one 7.92mm (0.31in) Besa machine gun
POWERPLANT: 1 x Bedford twin-six petrol engine developing 350hp (261kW)
PERFORMANCE: maximum road speed 20km/h (12.5mph); maximum cross-country speed about 12.8km/h (8mph); fording 1.02m (3ft 4in); vertical obstacle 0.76m (2ft 6in); trench 3.05m (10ft)

ARK

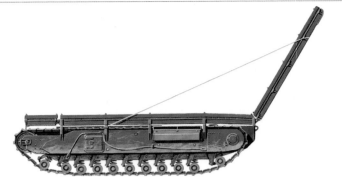

The British Army produced its first bridging tank at the end of World War I and experimented throughout the interwar period, seeing the need to have vehicles to facilitate the crossing of obstacles. The first Armoured Ramp Carrier, the ARK Mk I, appeared in 1943. This was a converted Churchill tank with the turret removed, a blanking plate welded over the aperture and timbered trackways across the top. The ARK could be driven into ditches or against obstacles and, when the two folding ramps were lowered, it could be used as a bridge for other vehicles. Variants included the Churchill Woodlark, which used rockets to open up the ramps and put them into position, and the Churchill Great Eastern, which used a raised ramp system, but neither was very successful.

SPECIFICATIONS

COUNTRY OF ORIGIN: United Kingdom
CREW: 4
WEIGHT: 38,385kg (84,450lb)
DIMENSIONS: length 7.44m (24ft 5in); width 2.43m (7ft 11in); height 2.13m (6ft 11in)
RANGE: 144km (90 miles)
ARMOUR: 16mm (0.63in)
ARMAMENT: none
POWERPLANT: 1 x Bedford twin-six petrol engine developing 350hp (261kW)
PERFORMANCE: maximum road speed 20km/h (12.5mph); maximum cross-country speed about 12.8km/h (8mph); fording 1.016m (3ft 4in); vertical obstacle 0.76m (2ft 6in); trench 3.05m (10ft)

Bergepanther

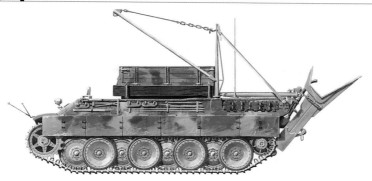

With the advent of the heavier Tiger and Panther tanks, standard German recovery vehicles such as the SdKfz 9/1 proved inadequate. The Panther tank was therefore used as the basis for a new heavy recovery vehicle. The Bergepanther first appeared in 1943. The Panther's turret was removed and replaced by an open superstructure containing a winch. A large anchor at the back dug into the ground to give the vehicle extra stability when winching. There was also an open machine-gun mounting on the front of the vehicle for self-defence. Bergepanthers entered full service in the spring of 1944, concentrated in the heavy tank battalions, and, by the end of the war, almost 300 had been produced. It proved to be the best recovery vehicle of World War II.

SPECIFICATIONS

COUNTRY OF ORIGIN: Germany
CREW: 5
WEIGHT: 42,000kg (92,400lb)
DIMENSIONS: length 8.153m (26ft 9in); width 3.276m (10ft 9in); height 2.74m (8ft 11in)
RANGE: 169km (105 miles)
ARMOUR: 8–40mm (0.3–1.57in)
ARMAMENT: 1 x 20mm (0.79in) cannon and one 7.92mm (0.31in) machine gun
POWERPLANT: 1 x Maybach HL210 P.30 petrol engine developing 642hp (478.7kW)
PERFORMANCE: maximum road speed 32km/h (20mph); fording 1.70m (5ft 7in); vertical obstacle 0.91m (2ft 11in); trench 1.91m (6ft 3in)

Carden-Loyd Mk VI

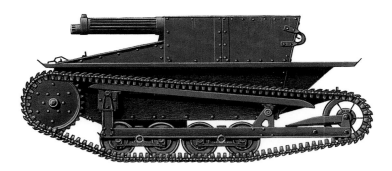

Carden-Loyd tankettes were an unsuccessful interwar experiment in providing armoured mobile machine-gun carriers for pairs of infantrymen. The first tankette was produced in 1925, a small tracked vehicle big enough for one man only, subsequently topped with a flimsy shield and a Hotchkiss machine gun to form the Carden-Loyd Mk I. Several variations were then produced, focusing mainly on experiments with track and suspension configurations. In 1926, a two-man version was produced, which became the Vickers machine-gun-armed Carden-Loyd Mk VI in 1928. Two more versions emerged and achieved some sales abroad, but the vehicles were tactically impractical and had no future past the mid-1930s.

SPECIFICATIONS

COUNTRY OF ORIGIN: United Kingdom
CREW: 2
WEIGHT: 1600kg (3500lb)
DIMENSIONS: length 2.47m (8ft 1in); width 1.7m (5ft 6in); height 1.22m (4ft)
RANGE: 160km (199 miles)
ARMOUR: 9mm (0.35in) maximum
ARMAMENT: 1 x 7.7mm (0.30in) Vickers MG
POWERPLANT: 1 x Ford T 4-cylinder petrol, developing 40hp (30kW)
PERFORMANCE: maximum road speed: 45km/h (28mph)

Bren Gun Carrier

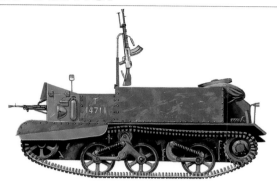

The Bren Carrier was more correctly known as the Universal (Bren Gun) Carrier. Produced between 1934 and 1960, it was used to transport a two-man Bren gun team, though initially it was designed as a gun tractor for a Vickers machine gun and a four-man crew. It was the advent of the Bren gun in 1936 that put an end to its gun tractor days. In effect, the Carrier was little more than an armoured metal box. The engine was placed in the centre of the vehicle next to the driver and gunner; the noise was apparently deafening. Despite their crudity, the Carriers were much used, and around 10 could be found in each infantry battalion. Various experimental models abounded, including versions mounting 25-pounder (87.6mm/3.45in) guns.

SPECIFICATIONS

COUNTRY OF ORIGIN: United Kingdom
CREW: 2
WEIGHT: 4000kg (8818lb)
DIMENSIONS: length 3.65m (11ft 11in); width 2.11m (6ft 11in); height 1.57m (5ft 2in)
RANGE: 250km (155 miles)
ARMOUR: 10mm (0.39in) maximum
ARMAMENT: 1 x 7.62mm (0.3in) Bren MG
POWERPLANT: 1 x Ford V-8 petrol, developing 85hp (63kW) at 3500rpm
PERFORMANCE: maximum road speed 48km/h (30mph)

P 107

The P 107 came in two basic variants: an artillery tractor for light field pieces and an engineer tractor. The latter had an open cargo body behind the cab and was used to tow trailers carrying combat engineer equipment. Following the fall of France to the Germans in 1940, the P 107 was pressed into Wehrmacht service, being used to tow field and anti-tank guns. Then the Germans stripped the vehicles of their superstructures and fitted armoured hulls in their place. Most of these conversions remained in France for training purposes and general duties, though they did see combat following the D-Day landings in June 1944. The Germans retained the mounted roller under the nose of the vehicle, which was used to assist the vehicle in and out of ditches.

SPECIFICATIONS

COUNTRY OF ORIGIN: France
CREW: 2 + 5
WEIGHT: 4050kg (8929lb)
DIMENSIONS: length 4.85m (15ft 11in); width 1.80m (5ft 11in); height 1.95m (6ft 5in)
RANGE: 400km (249 miles)
ARMOUR: (original version)
ARMAMENT: none
POWERPLANT: 1 x 4-cylinder petrol engine developing 55hp (41.0kW)
PERFORMANCE: maximum road speed 45km/h (28mph)

SdKfz 2

The SdKfz 2 was developed for use by German infantry and airborne units. It was designed to be an artillery tractor for very light weaponry. Known as the Kettenkrad, the first of these small tractors entered service in 1941. However, by this time German airborne troops were generally being used as regular infantry, so the vehicle's intended role was largely redundant. As a result, the SdKfz 2 was used mainly as a supply vehicle in difficult terrain, where other vehicles could not travel. Their impact was limited by their low cargo capacity and limited production numbers. By 1944, they were seen as an expensive luxury and production ceased. One interesting variant was a high-speed cable-laying vehicle for linking command posts and forward positions.

SPECIFICATIONS

COUNTRY OF ORIGIN: Germany
CREW: 3
WEIGHT: 1200kg (2646lb)
DIMENSIONS: length 2.74m (8ft 11in); width 1m (3ft 3in); height 1.01m (3ft 4in)
RANGE: 100km (62.14 miles)
ARMOUR: none
ARMAMENT: none
POWERPLANT: 1 x Opel Olympia 38 petrol engine developing 36hp (26.8kW)
PERFORMANCE: maximum road speed 80km/h (49.7mph)

SdKfz 7

Development of the SdKfz 7 can be traced back to a 1934 requirement for an 8-tonne (7.8-ton) halftrack. The vehicle first appeared in 1938 and was destined to be used mainly as the tractor for the 8.8cm (3.46in) flak guns. The vehicle could carry up to 12 men and a considerable quantity of supplies, as well as pulling up to 8000kg (17,637lb). Most were fitted with a winch, and the vehicle was widely admired as a useful vehicle, being also used as a weapons carrier, to particularly good effect with anti-aircraft weapons. They also saw service as observation and command posts for V2 rocket batteries. They were admired even by their enemies, with the British trying to make exact copies of captured vehicles and some vehicles being appropriated for use by the Allies after World War II.

SPECIFICATIONS

COUNTRY OF ORIGIN: Germany
CREW: 12
WEIGHT: 11,550kg (25,463lb)
DIMENSIONS: length 6.85m (20ft 3in); width 2.40m (7ft 11in); height 2.62m (8ft 7in)
RANGE: 250km (155 miles)
ARMOUR: 8mm (0.31in)
ARMAMENT: (basic version) none
POWERPLANT: 1 x Maybach HL 62 6-cylinder petrol engine developing 140hp (104.4kW)
PERFORMANCE: maximum road speed 50km/h (31mph); fording 0.5m (1ft 8in); vertical obstacle 2.0m (6ft 7in)

SdKfz 9

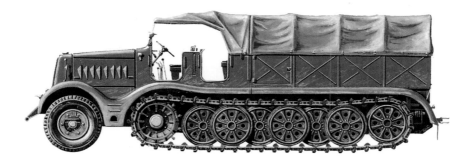

The SdKfz 9 was by far the largest of all World War II halftracks. It originated as a result of a 1936 requirement for a heavy recovery vehicle to operate alongside Panzer units. The vehicle was used both for recovery and for towing heavy artillery and bridging units. A weapons-carrying version was produced in 1943 mounting an 8.8cm (3.46in) anti-aircraft gun, where it saw action in Poland and France. The recovery version was fitted with a crane and stabilizing legs to allow it to cope with heavy tanks. However, even with an earth spade at the back for extra traction, two SdKfz 9s were generally required to recover tanks such as the massive Tiger, and when the more capable Bergepanther arrived the SdKfz's role was diminished somewhat and therefore production ceased in 1944.

SPECIFICATIONS

COUNTRY OF ORIGIN: Germany
CREW: 9
WEIGHT: 18,000kg (39,683lb)
DIMENSIONS: length 8.25m (27ft 1in); width 2.60m (8ft 6in); height 2.76m (9ft 1in)
RANGE: 260km (162 miles)
ARMOUR: 8–14.5mm (0.31–0.57in)
ARMAMENT: none, though sometimes 1 x 8.8cm (3.46in) Flak gun
POWERPLANT: 1 x Maybach HL V-12 petrol engine developing 250hp (186.4kW)
PERFORMANCE: maximum road speed 50km/h (31mph); fording 0.6m (1ft 11in); vertical obstacle 2.0m (6ft 7in)

SdKfz 10/4

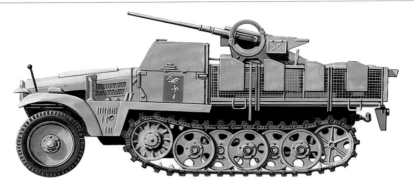

The SdKfz 10 was a general light utility vehicle/troop transporter introduced into the German armed forces in 1937. As an artillery tractor, it was used to draw weapons such as the 370mm (14.6in) PaK 35/36 or the 150mm (5.9in) sIG 33 field gun. It could also carry eight fully armed soldiers. Over 17,000 SdKfz 10s were produced between 1938 and the end of World War II, and many variants were designed for combat roles. The SdKfz 10/4, for example, was an anti-aircraft model. It initially mounted a single-barrel 20mm (0.78in) Flak 30 cannon, though many were subsequently upgraded to the Flak 38. The sides and rear of the hull could be folded flat to create an operating platform for the gun crew.

SPECIFICATIONS

COUNTRY OF ORIGIN: Germany
CREW: 7
WEIGHT: 4900kg (10,800lb)
DIMENSIONS: length 4.75m (15ft 7in); width 1.93m (6ft 4in); height 1.62m (5ft 4in)
RANGE: 300km (186 miles)
ARMOUR: (steel) 14.5mm (0.57in) maximum
ARMAMENT: 1 x 20mm (0.79in) Flak 30 or Flak 38 cannon
POWERPLANT: 1 x Maybach HL 42 TRKM 6-cylinder petrol, developing 100hp (75kW)
PERFORMANCE: maximum road speed: 65km/h (40mph)

SdKfz 11

The first versions of the SdKfz 11 appeared in 1934 and after a series of manufacturing changes, the vehicle entered full production in 1939. Primarily intended as an artillery tractor, it was used initially by 10.5cm (4.13in) howitzer batteries. The vehicle proved so successful that it was later used to tow a wide variety of guns at the expense of heavier purpose-built vehicles, eventually seeing most service with Nebelwerfer batteries to tow the rocket launchers. The vehicle was one of the few to remain in production right through the war, and a number of variants were produced, including two designed specifically for chemical warfare decontamination, but these were not produced in significant numbers as large-scale chemical warfare never occurred during World War II.

SPECIFICATIONS

COUNTRY OF ORIGIN: Germany
CREW: 9
WEIGHT: 7100kg (15,653lb)
DIMENSIONS: length 5.48m (17ft 11in); width 1.82m (5ft 11in); height 1.62m (5ft 4in)
RANGE: 122km (76 miles)
ARMOUR: 8–14mm (0.31–0.55in)
ARMAMENT: none
POWERPLANT: 1 x 6-cylinder petrol engine developing 100hp (74.6kW)
PERFORMANCE: maximum road speed 53km/h (33mph); fording 0.75m (2ft 6in); vertical obstacle 2.0m (6ft 7in)

SdKfz 250/3

The basic SdKfz 250 was a one-ton halftrack with an armoured hull and an open-top crew compartment occupying approximately half of the vehicle. It was one of the first halftracks used by Germany in World War II, and 6000 were produced during the course of the war. It was conceived as an infantry carrier and support vehicle, and had a crew of six, armed with two 7.92mm (0.31in) MG34 or MG42 machine guns. The first version, the SdKfz 250/1, was only the first among 10 subsequent variants. The SdKfz 250/3 Leichter Funkpanzerwagen was an FuG12radio vehicle used to control and coordinate motorized units. It was mounted with a large 2m (6ft 7in) rod aerial, and later a 2m (6ft 7in) star aerial.

SPECIFICATIONS

COUNTRY OF ORIGIN: Germany
CREW: 6
WEIGHT: 5340kg (11,775lb)
DIMENSIONS: length 4.56m (14ft 11in); width 1.95m (6ft 5in); height 1.66m (5ft 5in)
RANGE: 350km (217 miles)
ARMOUR: (steel) 15mm (0.59in) maximum
ARMAMENT: 1 x 7.92mm (0.31in) MG34 MG
POWERPLANT: 1 x Maybach hL 42 6-cylinder diesel, developing 120hp (89kW) at 3000rpm
PERFORMANCE: maximum road speed 65km/h (40mph); fording 0.75m (2ft 6in); gradient 24 per cent

SdKfz 250/10

The SdKfz 250 was developed following a mid-1930's requirement for a 1-tonne (0.9-ton) halftrack to provide mobility for infantry and other units operating with panzer divisions. The first example appeared in 1939 and saw action for the first time in May 1940 during the invasion of France. Production continued until 1944, with later models having redesigned hulls to make manufacture easier and cut down on the amount of raw materials required, as the basic design was rather expensive. Variants included a communications vehicle and mobile observation post, as well as a number of specialised weapons carriers, mounting everything from anti-aircraft guns to anti-tank cannons. The vehicle remained in service until the end of the war proving to be a reliable and popular halftrack.

SPECIFICATIONS

COUNTRY OF ORIGIN: Germany
CREW: 6
WEIGHT: 5380kg (11,861lb)
DIMENSIONS: length 4.56m (14ft 11in); width 1.95m (6ft 5in); height 1.98m (6ft 6in)
RANGE: 299km (186 miles)
ARMOUR: 6–14.5mm (0.23–0.6in)
ARMAMENT: 1 x 3.7cm (1.37in) Pak 35/36 anti-tank gun
POWERPLANT: 1 x six-cylinder petrol engine developing 100hp (74.6kW)
PERFORMANCE: maximum road speed 59.5km/h (37mph); fording 0.75m (2ft 6in); vertical obstacle 2.0m (6ft 7in)

SdKfz 251/1

The SdKfz 251 had its origins in the same requirement as the SdKfz 250. However, the 251 series was a heavier vehicle. It entered service in 1939, intended as an armoured personnel carrier. The 250 was a useful vehicle, capable of keeping up with Panzer formations. There were 22 special-purpose variants, including rocket-launcher (referred to as the 'infantry Stuka'), flame-thrower, anti-tank, communications vehicle, observation post and ambulance and infrared searchlight carrier. Early reliability problems did not prevent the vehicle being produced by the thousands, and it was a sturdy vehicle used on all fronts, becoming a virtual trademark of German Panzer formations. The SdKfz 251/1 was the standard armoured personnel carrier for the Panzergrenadier group.

SPECIFICATIONS

COUNTRY OF ORIGIN: Germany
CREW: 12
WEIGHT: 7810kg (17,218lb)
DIMENSIONS: length 5.80m (19ft); width 2.10m (6ft 11in); height 1.75m (5ft 9in)
RANGE: 300km (186 miles)
ARMOUR: 6–14.5mm (0.23–0.6in)
ARMAMENT: 2 x 7.92mm (0.31in) machine guns
POWERPLANT: 1 x Maybach 6-cylinder petrol engine developing 100hp (74.6kW)
PERFORMANCE: maximum road speed 52.5km/h (32.5mph); fording 0.6m (1ft 11in); vertical obstacle 2.0m (6ft 7in)

SdKfz 251 Wurfkörper

Wurfkörper 28cm (11in) and 32cm (12.6in) rockets were amongst the first to be fitted to vehicles to provide mobile firepower. The vehicle most often used was the SdKfz 251, this combination being known as the Stuka-zu-fuss ('Foot Stuka') or Heulende Kuh ('Howling Cow'). The combination saw action through World War II. The system was rather temperamental, as the rockets were highly inaccurate and aiming was achieved by simply pointing the vehicle in the general direction of the target. As a result, they tended to be used en masse where possible. They were still devastating weapons whenever they did hit the target, the high-explosive warhead being particularly well regarded for street fighting and demolishing houses. The specifications here relate to the Wurfkörper M FI 50 rocket.

SPECIFICATIONS

COUNTRY OF ORIGIN: Germany
CREW: 6
WEIGHT: 9000kg (19.842lb)
DIMENSIONS: length 5.98m (19ft 7in); width 2.1m (6ft 11in); height 2.16m (7ft 1in)
RANGE: 300km (186 miles)
ARMOUR: (steel) 15mm (0.59in) maximum
ARMAMENT: 6 x 28cm (11in) unguided rockets
POWERPLANT: 1 x Maybach hL 42 6-cylinder diesel, developing 100hp (74.5kW)
PERFORMANCE: maximum road speed: 53km/h (33mph)

M3 Halftrack

American halftrack production began in earnest in 1941, and by the end of the war over 40,000 of all types had been produced. The M3 was widely used by all Allied forces, mainly as a personnel carrier, although also saw service as an ambulance, communications vehicle and artillery tractor. In fact, it was so prolific that it became something of a trademark of Allied forces, particularly after the D-Day landings of June 1944. After World War II, the M3 was gradually reduced to the role of recovery vehicle. However, vehicles supplied to the Soviet Union before 1945 continued to see service with some Warsaw Pact countries for many years. It also remained a frontline vehicle for the Israeli Defence Force until relatively recently, seeing service in all the Arab-Israeli wars.

SPECIFICATIONS

COUNTRY OF ORIGIN: United States
CREW: 13
WEIGHT: 9299kg (20,501lb)
DIMENSIONS: length 6.18m (20ft 3in); width 2.22m (7ft 3in); height 2.26m (7ft 5in)
RANGE: 282km (175 miles)
ARMOUR: 8mm (0.31in)
ARMAMENT: 1 x 12.7mm (0.5in) machine gun; 1 x 7.62mm (0.3in) machine gun
POWERPLANT: 1 x White 160AX 6-cylinder petrol engine developing 147hp (109.6kW)
PERFORMANCE: maximum road speed 64.4km/h (40mph); fording 0.81m (2ft 8in)

Maultier

German trucks proved totally unable of operating successfully during the first winter of the Russian campaign in 1941–1942. It was thus decided to produce a low-cost halftrack to take over many of the trucks' duties. The Wehrmachtsschlepper could not be produced in sufficient numbers to fulfil this need so Opel and Daimler-Benz chassis were fixed to tracked assemblies from PzKpfw II tanks. The new Maultier as it was known was a reasonable success, although lacking the mobility of 'proper' halftracks. By late 1942, the Maultier was being pressed into service as a launch-vehicle for the Nebelwerfer rocket launcher, with over 3000 conversions being ordered by the German Army. In combat Maultiers were organized into Nebelwerfer brigades.

SPECIFICATIONS

COUNTRY OF ORIGIN: Germany
CREW: 3
WEIGHT: 7100kg (15,620lb)
DIMENSIONS: length 6m (19ft 8in); width 2.20m (7ft 3in); height 2.50m (8ft 6in)
RANGE: 130km (81 miles)
ARMOUR: 8–10mm (0.31–0.39in)
ARMAMENT: 1 x 15cm (5.9in) Nebelwerfer (later versions); one 7.92mm (0.31in) machine gun
POWERPLANT: 1 x 3.6-litre six-cylinder petrol engine developing 91hp (68kW)
PERFORMANCE: maximum road speed 38km/h (30mph); fording 0.6m (1ft 11in); vertical obstacle 2.0m (6ft 7in); trench 1m (3ft 3in)

Schwerer Wehrmachtsschlepper

By 1941, the German Army was in need of a medium halftrack, but it had to be economical to produce as the German war machine was already stretched. The Schwerer Wehrmachtsschlepper, or army heavy tractor, was intended for use by infantry units as a general supply vehicle and personnel carrier. To keep costs down, luxuries like a closed cab and rubber-capped tracks were mainly dispensed with. Production was slow, partly due to the lack of priority accorded the vehicle and partly due to the attentions of RAF Bomber Command. However, production continued until the end of the World War II, with a few vehicles seeing service in the post-war Czech Army. Variants included a rocket launcher, anti-aircraft vehicle and a frontline supply vehicle fitted with an armoured cab.

SPECIFICATIONS

COUNTRY OF ORIGIN: Germany
CREW: 2
WEIGHT: 13,500kg (29,762lb)
DIMENSIONS: length 6.68m (21ft 11in); width 2.50m (8ft 2in); height 2.83m (9ft 3in)
RANGE: 300km (186 miles)
ARMOUR: 8–15mm (0.31–0.59in)
ARMAMENT: 1 x 3.7cm (1.46in) gun; 1 x 7.92mm (0.31in) machine gun
POWERPLANT: 1 x Maybach HL 42 6-cylinder petrol engine developing 100hp (74.6kW)
PERFORMANCE: maximum road speed 27km/h (16.8mph); fording 0.6m (1ft 11in); vertical obstacle 2.0m (6ft 7in)

Panzerwerfer 42

The 15cm Panzerwerfer 42 (SdKfz 4/1) was a self-propelled version of the German 15cm (5.9in) Nebelwerfer rocket system. Opel was commissioned to build the vehicle in 1943 and did so by taking Opel and Daimler-Benz light trucks, removing their rear axles, and replacing them with the tracked assemblies from PzKpfw IIs. A fully armed superstructure protected the crew of four men, with a maximum armour thickness of 10mm (0.39in). The 10-barrelled Nebelwerfer 42 was set on the roof on a turntable fitting which could traverse 270 degrees and elevate 80 degrees. Secondary armament consisted of a single 7.92mm (0.31in) MG34 or MG42 machine gun. The Panzerwerfer 42 was mainly used on the Eastern Front from 1943.

SPECIFICATIONS

COUNTRY OF ORIGIN: Germany
CREW: 4
WEIGHT: 7100kg (15,653lb)
DIMENSIONS: length 6.02m (19ft 9in); width 2.26m (7ft 5in); height 2.17m (7ft 1in)
RANGE: not available
ARMOUR: (steel) 10mm (0.39in) maximum
ARMAMENT: 1 x Nebelwerfer 42 rocket launcher; 1 x 7.92mm (0.31in) MG34 or MG42 machine gun
POWERPLANT: 1 x Opel Olympia 6-cylinder petrol, developing 67hp (50kW)
PERFORMANCE: maximum road speed: 40km/h (25mph)

Ram Kangaroo

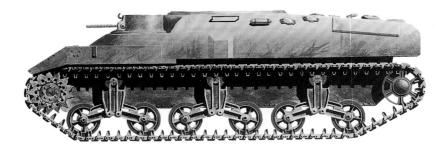

The Ram/Kangaroo was an expedient vehicle used to transport Canadian soldiers into action in Europe in late 1944. The vehicle was essentially a turretless Canadian Ram tank, which was developed in 1942 and 1943 but was quickly rendered obsolete by the introduction of the US Sherman tank. By mid-1944, 500 Rams were in storage in England, and these were converted into armoured personnel carriers. The turret was removed, benches were fixed in the interior alongside ammunition racks and a standard infantry No.19 wireless set was fitted. Ram/Kangaroos were light and mobile vehicles, and joined the ranks of several similar Allied tank conversions.

SPECIFICATIONS

COUNTRY OF ORIGIN: Canada/United Kingdom
CREW: 2 + 8
WEIGHT: 29,000kg (63,900lb)
DIMENSIONS: Length: 5.79m (19ft); width: 2.78m (9.12ft); height: 2.47m (8.1ft)
RANGE: 230km (140 miles)
ARMOUR: 88mm (3.46in) maximum
ARMAMENT: 1 x 7.62mm (0.3in) MG
POWERPLANT: 1 x Continental R-975 9-cylinder diesel, developing 399hp (298kW)
PERFORMANCE: Maximum road speed: 40km/h (25mph); vertical obstacle: 0.6m (2ft); trench: 2.26m (7.41ft)

Morris C8

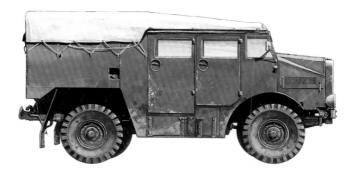

The Morris C8 artillery tractor was one of the most successful of the range of vehicles produced by Morris for the British Army. Popularly known as the Quad, the vehicle was introduced in 1939. It was used to tow the 18- or 25-pounder gun and was equipped with a winch, which could lift loads of up to 4000kg (8818lb). Inside there was room for the gun crew. The Morris C8 was a sturdy vehicle with good cross-country mobility and adequate stowage space for ammunition. Early models had a distinctive beetle shape, but from 1944 onwards the vehicle was fitted with an open top. A large number of C8s were lost during the British Expeditionary Force's withdrawal from Dunkirk in 1940, but the vehicle did go on to see service in North Africa. Transmission consisted of five forward and one reverse gears.

SPECIFICATIONS

COUNTRY OF ORIGIN: United Kingdom
CREW: 1
WEIGHT: 3402kg (7500lb)
DIMENSIONS: length 4.49m (14ft 9in); width 2.21m (7ft 3in); height 2.26m (7ft 5in)
RANGE: 480km (298 miles)
ARMOUR: none
ARMAMENT: none
POWERPLANT: 1 x Morris 4-cylinder 3.5-litre petrol engine developing 70hp (52.2kW)
PERFORMANCE: maximum road speed 80km/h (50mph); fording 0.4m (1ft 4in)

Stöwer 40

In 1934, the Germans began to create standardized vehicles for the Wehrmacht in preparation for the inevitable war in Europe. Up until then, cross-country vehicles had been based on commercial designs, with all their disadvantages with relation to military uses. The new method would involve taking into account not only technical but operational considerations when designing a vehicle. The Kfz 2 entered production in 1936, based on a number of different manufacturers' components, including Stöwer, BMW and Hanomag. A 4 x 4 design, it was often used as the basis for radio cars. The chassis was normal, except for additional bracing on the engine, suspension and transmission for strength. The Stöwer 40 had five forward and one reverse gears, and was a solid and reliable vehicle.

SPECIFICATIONS

COUNTRY OF ORIGIN: Germany
CREW: 1
WEIGHT: 1815kg (4001lb)
DIMENSIONS: length 3.58m (11ft 9in); width 1.57m (5ft 2in); height 1.78m (5ft 10in)
RANGE: 500km (311 miles)
ARMOUR: none
ARMAMENT: none
POWERPLANT: 1 x Stower AW2 or R180W 4-cylinder OHV petrol engine developing 50hp (37.3kW)
PERFORMANCE: maximum road speed 100km/h (62.5mph); fording 0.6m (1ft 11in)

Dodge T215

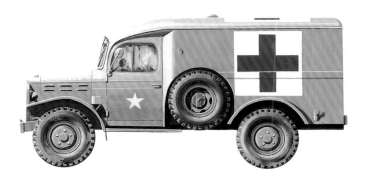

odge was the sole provider of ½-ton trucks for the US Army. The order for 14,000 was made in mid-1940. Dodge altered the basic commercial chassis slightly for military use, giving it four-wheel drive. There was the option of an open cab (as with the command, reconnaissance, radio and weapons carrier versions) or fixed bodywork as with the ambulance). The Dodge was a sturdy vehicle manufactured in large numbers, many of which were shipped to the United Kingdom and Soviet Union under the Lend-Lease scheme of World War II. Interestingly, the Russians were less than impressed with the tanks supplied by the British and Americans under the scheme, but they were very grateful when it came to the jeeps and lorries supplied, using them for many years after the end of the war.

SPECIFICATIONS

COUNTRY OF ORIGIN: United States
CREW: 1
WEIGHT: 2046kg (4501lb)
DIMENSIONS: length 4.67m (15ft 4in); width 1.93m (6ft 4in); height 2.13m (7ft 0in)
RANGE: 500km (311 miles)
ARMOUR: none
ARMAMENT: none
POWERPLANT: 1 x Dodge T215 6-cylinder petrol engine developing 92hp (68.6kW)
PERFORMANCE: maximum road speed 70km/h (43.75mph); fording 0.6m (1ft 11in)

Dodge WC53

The Dodge T214 WC53 Command and Reconnaissance Vehicle was used in a very similar way to the ubiquitous Jeep. The most common variant of the Dodge T214 series, it was used for reconnaissance (as its name suggests) and for liaising between different units. It also served as a staff vehicle for high-ranking officers. The vehicle was fitted with map boards and had a detachable canvas top and side-screens. A good all-round utility vehicle, reliable and mobile, it served in all theatres of the war. One of its greatest attributes was its Dodge six-cylinder petrol engine, which could withstand poor maintenance, hard treatment and a variety of adverse weather conditions. In addition, the chassis was able to take on most types of terrain, from the humid jungles of the Pacific to the snows of northern Europe.

SPECIFICATIONS

COUNTRY OF ORIGIN: United States
CREW: 1
WEIGHT: 2449kg (5399lb)
DIMENSIONS: length 4.24m (13ft 11in); width 1.99m (6ft 6in); height 2.07m (6ft 9in)
RANGE: 450km (281 miles)
ARMOUR: none
ARMAMENT: none
POWERPLANT: 1 x Dodge T214 6-cylinder petrol engine developing 92hp (68.6kW)
PERFORMANCE: maximum road speed 110km/h (68.75mph); fording 0.5m (1ft 7in)

Jeep

In June 1940, the US Army issued a requirement for a 'go-anywhere' vehicle. After initial design changes, Ford and Willys both began production of the Jeep and between them manufactured nearly 650,000 vehicles. Intended for reconnaissance and liaison duties, the Jeep was so successful that it was soon adapted for other duties, including airborne landings and for use as rocket-launchers. They were adapted by the British SAS for long-range desert raids, mainly by being stripped of luxuries and heavily armed. Jeeps were used as ambulances and for laying telephone lines. If fitted with special flanged wheels, the Jeep could even travel along railway lines. Adapted for different climactic conditions, the Jeep served with distinction in all Allied theatres.

SPECIFICATIONS

COUNTRY OF ORIGIN: United States
CREW: 1
WEIGHT: 1247kg (2749lb)
DIMENSIONS: length 3.33m (10ft 11in); width 1.57m (5ft 2in); height 1.14m (3ft 9in)
RANGE: 363km (225 miles)
ARMOUR: none
ARMAMENT: none (basic model)
POWERPLANT: 1 x Willys 441 or 442 'Go Devil' 4-cylinder petrol engine developing 60hp (44.7kW)
PERFORMANCE: maximum road speed 88.5km/h (55mph); fording 0.5m (1ft 7in)

VW Kübel

The Kübel was one of the most famous military cars of World War II, and became something of a trademark with German forces in the conflict. Development began in 1936 and, following design changes to accommodate more requirements, when it was announced that it would be the standard personnel carrier of the army, production began in 1940. The two main design considerations were lightness and ease of manufacture. It was also very cheap to make. Reliable, mobile and simple to maintain, the vehicle met all the demands made on it. By the time production ceased in 1944, some 55,000 had been made. Variants included the Type 92 with an enclosed body. In the desert the vehicle performed poorly, but a way round this was found in the Tropenfest version, which was equipped with sand tyres.

SPECIFICATIONS

COUNTRY OF ORIGIN: Germany
CREW: 1
WEIGHT: 635kg (1397lb)
DIMENSIONS: length 3.73m (12ft 3in); width 1.60m (5ft 3in); height 1.35m (4ft 5in)
RANGE: 600km (373 miles)
ARMOUR: none
ARMAMENT: none
POWERPLANT: 1 x Volkswagen 14-cylinder HIAR 998cc petrol engine developing 24hp (17.9kW), or (from March 1943) 1 x Volkswagen 4-cylinder 1131cc petrol engine developing 25hp (18.6kW)
PERFORMANCE: maximum road speed 100km/h (62.5mph); fording 0.4m (1ft 4in)

Ford C11 ADF

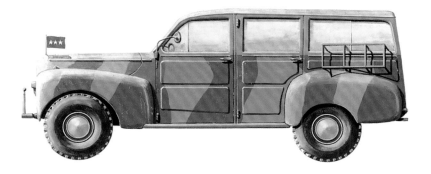

The Ford C11 ADF was based on the commercial 1942 Ford Fordor Station Wagon. Produced mainly for the British (and fitted with right-hand drive for this purpose), but also used by the Canadian Army, the vehicle saw extensive service as a staff vehicle in the Western Desert and Italy. The all-steel body had space for five passengers. The vehicle was fitted with strengthened bumpers, internal rifle racks, entrenching tools and radio-interference suppression equipment, as well as a full medical kit and map containers. In short, it was adequately equipped to allow staff officers to operate it as a mobile command centre. It was also rugged enough to stand up to the adverse terrain of North Africa. Transmission consisted of three forward and one reverse gears.

SPECIFICATIONS

COUNTRY OF ORIGIN: Canada
CREW: 1
WEIGHT: 1814kg (3999lb)
DIMENSIONS: length 4.93m (16ft 2in); width 2.01m (6ft 7in); height 1.83m (6ft 0in)
RANGE: 500km (311 miles)
ARMOUR: none
ARMAMENT: none
POWERPLANT: 1 x Ford mercury V-8 3.91-litre petrol engine developing 95hp (70.8kW)
PERFORMANCE: maximum road speed 90km/h (56mph); fording 0.4m (1ft 4in)

Humber Heavy Utility Car

The Humber Heavy Utility Car was the standard staff and command car of the British Army during World War II (the army was the only fully motorized force when war broke out in September 1939). It was also the only 4 x 4 British-built four-wheel drive utility car employed. Production of the 'Box' began in May 1941 and continued until 1945. Widely used, the vehicle remained in service until the late 1950s – testimony to the quality of its design. Its fixed steel bodywork carried six seats and a folding map table. In the desert, the fixed cab was sometimes replaced by a canvas cover. The Humber was unspectacular in design, but more importantly it did the job required of it, and in different theatres. Transmission consisted of four forward and one reverse gears.

SPECIFICATIONS

COUNTRY OF ORIGIN: United Kingdom
CREW: 1
WEIGHT: 2413kg (5319lb)
DIMENSIONS: length 4.29m (14ft 1in); width 1.88m (6ft 2in); height 1.96m (6ft 5in) x
RANGE: 500km (311 miles)
ARMOUR: none
ARMAMENT: none
POWERPLANT: 1 x Humber 6-cylinder 1-L-W-F 4.08-litre petrol engine developing 85hp (63.4kW)
PERFORMANCE: maximum road speed 75km/h (46.8mph); fording 0.6m (1ft 11in)

Dodge T214

Introduced in 1942, the Dodge T214 ¾-ton truck was the successor to the T215 and was slightly wider and lower with larger wheels and stronger suspensions. Referred to as 'Beeps' (a contraction of 'Big Jeeps'), the T214 had a range of body types for different roles: weapons carrier, winch-equipped, ambulance, radio vehicle, command reconnaissance vehicle and repair vehicle. The differences were mainly in the number of seats, map boards and type of canvas cover. The fact that many vehicles are still in use around the world today is a tribute to the sturdy design of these vehicles, which were characterized by an ability to take a lot of punishment and ease of maintenance. Transmission consisted of four forward and one reverse gears.

SPECIFICATIONS

COUNTRY OF ORIGIN: United States
CREW: 1
WEIGHT: 2449kg (5388lb)
DIMENSIONS: length 4.24m (13ft 11in); width 1.99m (6ft 6in); height 2.07m (6ft 9in)
RANGE: 450km (280 miles)
ARMOUR: none
ARMAMENT: none
POWERPLANT: 1 x Dodge T214 6-cylinder petrol engine developing 92hp (68.6kW)
PERFORMANCE: maximum road speed 110km/h (68.75mph); fording 0.5m (1ft 7in)

Daimler-Benz G5

The G series was developed to fill a Wehrmacht requirement for a personnel carrier with full cross-country capability. The first efforts by Daimler-Benz resulted in powerful vehicles with four-wheel drive and four-wheel steering, but their cross-country performance was poor. They were also too large and too expensive. Not chosen for production of the standard Einheit range of personnel carriers, Daimler-Benz continued to develop the G series. Between 1937 and 1941, 378 G5 vehicles were built, but few saw service with the Wehrmacht, although some were used as communications vehicles by high officials of the Nazi Party and the General Staff (an additional problem with many German light vehicles was that they were too complicated for reliability in rugged conditions, especially Russia).

SPECIFICATIONS

COUNTRY OF ORIGIN: Germany
CREW: 1
WEIGHT: 1630kg (3594lb)
DIMENSIONS: length 4.52m (14ft 10in); width 1.70m (5ft 7in); height 1.80m (5ft 11in)
RANGE: 480km (300 miles)
ARMOUR: none
ARMAMENT: none
POWERPLANT: 1 x Mercedes-Benz 6-cylinder petrol engine developing 90hp (67kW)
PERFORMANCE: maximum road speed 75km/h (46.8mph); fording 0.7m (2ft 4in)

Kraftfahrzeug (Kfz) 15

The main role of the Kfz 15 was as a communications vehicle. Powered by a V8 engine, the vehicle was based on a number of commercial chassis, including that of the Mercedes-Benz 340 chassis between 1938 and 1940. When the German Army was being rebuilt in the early 1930s, the theory was that that it should have specially built vehicles to carry out Blitzkrieg attacks. However, at first commercial car and light lorry chassis were used, with special bodies simply placed on top. The result was a whole series of poor military vehicles with low ground clearance. Thus the long wheelbase of this chassis tended to impair cross-country performance in spite of four-wheel drive. However, even after the introduction of the standard personnel carrier, many were used as staff cars and radio cars.

SPECIFICATIONS

COUNTRY OF ORIGIN: Germany
CREW: 1
WEIGHT: 2405kg (5302lb)
DIMENSIONS: length 4.44m (14ft 7in); width 1.68m (5ft 6in); height 1.73m (5ft 8in)
RANGE: 400km (249 miles)
ARMOUR: none
ARMAMENT: none
POWERPLANT: 1 x Mercedes-Benz 6-cylinder petrol engine developing 90hp (67.1kW)
PERFORMANCE: maximum road speed 88km/h (55mph); fording 0.6m (1ft 11in)

sIG 33

The sIG 33 was a self-propelled howitzer used to equip German infantry battalions of World War II. The first version appeared during the French Campaign of May 1940, and was simply the standard sIG 33 heavy infantry gun mounted on a PzKpfw I chassis and fitted with armoured shields to protect the crew. It was developed to provide armoured infantry with close fire support from a self-propelled armoured platform. The centre of gravity was rather high, though, and the chassis was overloaded. In consequence, the PzKpfw II chassis was converted for use in 1942, giving better armour protection, followed by the PzKpfw III. The vehicle served throughout the war and was still in production in 1944, with over 370 vehicles being made.

SPECIFICATIONS

COUNTRY OF ORIGIN: Germany
CREW: 4
WEIGHT: 11,505kg (25,364lb)
DIMENSIONS: length 4.84m (15ft 11in); width 2.15m (7ft 1in); height 2.40m (7ft 11in)
RANGE: 185km (115 miles)
ARMOUR: 6–13mm (0.23–0.5in)
ARMAMENT: 1 x 381mm (15cm) sIG 33 howitzer
POWERPLANT: 1 x Praga 6-cylinder petrol engine developing 150hp (111.9kW)
PERFORMANCE: maximum road speed 35km/h (21.75mph); fording 0.91m (3ft); vertical obstacle 0.42m (1ft 5in); trench 1.75m (5ft 9in)

Hummel

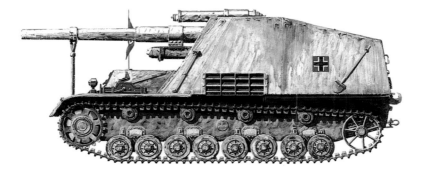

The Hummel ('Bumble Bee') was a hybrid of the PzKpfw III and IV hulls, with a lightly armoured open superstructure, which formed the heavy artillery element of German Panzer and Panzergrenadier divisions from 1942 onwards. The Hummel first saw action at the Battle of Kursk in July 1943. They were useful and popular weapons and were used on all fronts, having plenty of room for the crew of five and the mobility to keep up with the Panzer divisions. Well over 600 had been produced by late 1944, and 150 were converted into ammunition carriers as lorries proved inadequate for the task. Other variants included the Oskette, a wider-tracked version produced for winter fighting on the Russian Front. It was usual for 18 rounds of ammunition to be carried in the vehicle.

SPECIFICATIONS

COUNTRY OF ORIGIN: Germany
CREW: 5
WEIGHT: 23,927kg (52,750lb)
DIMENSIONS: length 7.17m (23ft 6in); width 2.87m (9ft 5in); height 2.81m (9ft 3in)
RANGE: 215km (134 miles)
ARMOUR: up to 50mm (1.97in)
ARMAMENT: 1 x 15cm (5.91in) sIG 33 howitzer or one 88mm (3.46in) anti-tank gun
POWERPLANT: 1 x Maybach V-12 petrol engine developing 265hp (197.6kW)
PERFORMANCE: maximum road speed 42km/h (26.1mph); fording 0.99m (3ft 3in); vertical obstacle 0.6m (1ft 11in); trench 2.20m (7ft 3in)

M7 Priest

Nicknamed the 'Priest' by British crews because of its pulpit-shaped machine-gun turret at the front, the M7 grew from US experience with howitzers mounted on halftracked vehicles. A fully tracked carriage was required, and the M3 tank was modified to fill the role. The British received many under the Lend-Lease scheme and deployed them first at the Second Battle of El Alamein in 1942. Some measure of their popularity is suggested by the British order for 5500 to be delivered within one year of their first use. The drawback was that the howitzer was not standard British issue, and thus required separate supplies of ammunition. Mobile and reliable, the M7 fought to the end of the war and remained in service in the role of armoured personnel carrier; it was also widely exported.

SPECIFICATIONS

COUNTRY OF ORIGIN: United States
CREW: 5
WEIGHT: 22,500kg (49,500lb)
DIMENSIONS: length 6.02m (19ft 9in); width 2.88m (9ft 5in); height 2.54m (8ft 4in)
RANGE: 201km (125 miles)
ARMOUR: up to 25.4mm (1in)
ARMAMENT: 1 x 105mm (4.13in) howitzer; 1 x 12.7mm (0.5in) machine gun
POWERPLANT: 1 x Continental 9-cylinder radial piston engine developing 375hp (279.6kW)
PERFORMANCE: maximum road speed 41.8km/h (26mph); fording 1.219m (4ft); vertical obstacle 0.61m (2ft); trench 1.91m (6ft 3in)

SU-76

The battles of 1941 showed the Soviet light tanks to be virtually useless. It was thus decided to combine the T-70 already in production with the excellent ZIS-3 and ZIS-76 guns to create a highly mobile anti-tank weapon. A wartime expedient, there were few comforts for the crew and it was known to troops as 'The Bitch'. The first SU-76s appeared in late 1942 and by mid-1943 they were deployed in appreciable numbers. Better German armour had by this time reduced the effectiveness of the ZIS gun and thus the vehicle's role was changed from anti-tank to infantry support. By 1945, many SU-76s were converted into ammunition carriers or recovery vehicles. After the war, many were transferred to China and North Korea, seeing service during the Korean War.

SPECIFICATIONS

COUNTRY OF ORIGIN: Soviet Union/Russia
CREW: 4
WEIGHT: 10,600kg (23,369lb)
DIMENSIONS: length 4.88m (16ft); width 2.73m (8ft 11in); height 2.17m (7ft 1in)
RANGE: 450km (280 miles)
ARMOUR: up to 25mm (0.98in)
ARMAMENT: 1 x ZIS-3 76mm gun
POWERPLANT: 2 x GAZ six-cylinder petrol engines each developing 70hp (52.2kW)
PERFORMANCE: maximum road speed 45km/h (28mph); fording 0.89m (2ft 11in); vertical obstacle 0.70m (2ft 4in); trench 3.12m (10ft 3in)

Sexton

In 1941, the British were searching for a suitable armoured vehicle to mount the standard British 25-pounder gun. The Canadians were producing the Ram tank, soon to be replaced by American M3s, and these were altered to accommodate the 25-pounder, becoming known as the Sexton. Used mainly as a field artillery weapon to support armoured divisions, the Sexton saw action in Northwest Europe in 1944 and 1945. By the time production ceased shortly after the war, a total of 2150 had been built. The main variant was a purpose-built command tank with the weapon removed and extra radios added. A reliable, rugged and effective weapon, the Sexton continued in service until the 1950s with the British Army, and until very recently with some other armies.

SPECIFICATIONS

COUNTRY OF ORIGIN: Canada
CREW: 6
WEIGHT: 25,300kg (55,777lb)
DIMENSIONS: length 6.12m (20ft 1in); width 2.72m (8ft 11in); height 2.44m (8ft)
RANGE: 290km (180 miles)
ARMOUR: up to 32mm (1.25in)
ARMAMENT: 1 x 25-pounder howitzer; 2 x 7.7mm (0.303in) Bren Guns; 1 x 12.7mm (0.5in) Browning machine gun
POWERPLANT: 1 x 9-cylinder radial piston engine developing 400hp (298.3kW)
PERFORMANCE: maximum road speed 40.2km/h (25mph); fording 1.01m (3ft 4in); vertical obstacle 0.61m (2ft); trench 1.91m (6ft 3in)

M41

The M41 was the only heavy tank destroyer produced by Italy during World War II. Using the chassis of the M14/41 tank, designers mounted a powerful antiaircraft gun on the vehicle. Designed to operate at long range, the M41 was not considered to require armour protection. The first production vehicles appeared in 1941, but only 48 were ever built, mainly because Italy's industrial plant was limited, but also because the gun was required for regular anti-aircraft duties. The M41 proved effective in the open spaces of North Africa, but after being seized by the Germans after the Italian surrender proved to have little value in the mountainous terrain of Italy, where few tanks could operate. Most were therefore used as long-range artillery.

SPECIFICATIONS

COUNTRY OF ORIGIN: Italy
CREW: 2 (on gun)
WEIGHT: 17,000kg (37,478lb)
DIMENSIONS: length 5.21m (17ft 1in); width 2.20m (7ft 3in); height 2.15m (7ft 1in)
RANGE: 200km (124 miles)
ARMOUR: none
ARMAMENT: 1 x 90mm (3.54in) cannon
POWERPLANT: 1 x SPA 15-TM-41 8-cylinder petrol engine developing 145hp (108.1kW)
PERFORMANCE: maximum road speed 35.5km/h (22mph); fording 1.0m (3ft 3in); vertical obstacle 0.9m (2ft 11in); trench 2.1m (6ft 11in)

L.40

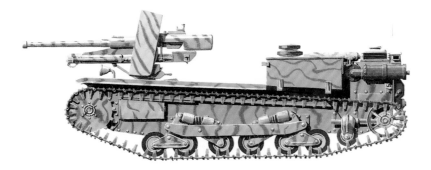

The Italians were ahead of tactical thinking in one aspect of armoured vehicle production, when they developed one of the first tank destroyers in the late 1930s. This thinking proved useful when it was realised that their light tanks were of little combat value in North Africa in 1941. The chassis of the Semovente M40 was fitted with a Böhler 47mm (1.85in) gun, one of the hardest hitting anti-tank weapons of its day. Around 280 of the tank destroyer vehicles were produced, and they fared adequately against Allied armour from 1942 onwards. Pressed into service by the Germans after the Italian surrender in 1943, the vehicle was unsuited for much of the Italian terrain and saw little action. Many had their armament removed and were converted into mobile command posts.

SPECIFICATIONS

COUNTRY OF ORIGIN: Italy
CREW: 2
WEIGHT: 6500kg (14,330lb)
DIMENSIONS: length 4.00m (13ft 2in); width 1.92m (6ft 4in); height 1.63m (5ft 4in)
RANGE: 200km (124 miles)
ARMOUR: 6–42mm (0.23–1.65in)
ARMAMENT: 1 x Böhler 47mm (1.85in) gun or 8mm (0.31in) Breda modelo 38 machine gun
POWERPLANT: 1 x SPA 18D four-cylinder petrol engine developing 68hp (50.7kW)
PERFORMANCE: maximum road speed 42.3km/h (26.3mph); fording 0.8m (2ft 7in); vertical obstacle 0.8m (2ft 7in); trench 1.7m (5ft 7in);

StuG III Ausf F

The StuG III Ausf F was developed from 1941, by personal order of Adolf Hitler himself, to regain superiority over the Soviet KV-1 and T-34 tanks on the Eastern Front. The armour of the Ausf A-E series was upgraded and a new long StuK40 L/48 7.5cm (2.95in) gun was fitted in place of the original short 7.5cm (2.95in) version, which significantly improved the vehicle's anti-tank capability. The basic hull and superstructure remained the same, other than the addition of an exhaust fan to remove gun fumes. The gun mantlet was also redesigned to allow for the recoil mechanism of the larger gun. The Ausf F proved highly effective against the Soviet KV-1s and T-34s and the vehicle remained in service throughout the war; its low silhouette gave it an added advantage in tank-versus-tank combats.

SPECIFICATIONS

COUNTRY OF ORIGIN: Germany
CREW: 4
WEIGHT: 21,800kg (48,061lb)
DIMENSIONS: length 6.31m (19ft 2in); width 2.92m (8ft 11in); height 2.15m (6ft 7in)
RANGE: 140km (92 miles)
ARMOUR: 11–50mm (0.4–2in)
ARMAMENT: 1 x 75mm (2.95in) Stuk40 L/48 gun; 1 x 7.92mm (0.31in) machine gun
POWERPLANT: 1 x Maybach HL120TRM engine
PERFORMANCE: maximum road speed 40km/h (25mph); fording 0.8m (2ft 8in); vertical obstacle 0.6m (1ft 11in); trench 2.59m (8ft 6in)

StuG III Ausf G

The StuG III Ausf G was the last StuG to enter production in World War II. Based predominantly on the chassis of the PzKpfw III, which was being phased out of tank service in favour of the much more lethal Panther, the Ausf G carried thicker armour than its predecessors, which was fortunate, as the Stug III was called upon more and more to fill the role of a tank, being cheaper and easier to build. However, its lack of mobility proved a liability as it was vulnerable to infantry with anti-tank projectiles. The addition of armoured 'skirts' (Schützen) went some way towards improving protection, but despite a valiant effort, the StuG IIIs were not really suited for the tank role in which they found themselves. Nevertheless, the Ausf G version was the best of the bunch, and performed well on the battlefield.

SPECIFICATIONS

COUNTRY OF ORIGIN: Germany
CREW: 4
WEIGHT: 24,100kg (53,131lb)
DIMENSIONS: length 6.77m (20ft 7in); width 2.95m (9ft 8in); height 2.16m (6ft 7in)
RANGE: 155km (97 miles)
ARMOUR: 16–80mm (0.62–3.14in)
ARMAMENT: 1 x 75mm (7.95in) Stuk40 L/48 gun; 1 x 7.92mm (0.31in) machine gun
POWERPLANT: 1 x Maybach HL120TRM engine
PERFORMANCE: maximum road speed 40km/h (25mph); fording 0.8m (2ft 8in); vertical obstacle 0.6m (2ft); trench 2.59m (8ft 6in)

M10

During the period immediately before its entry into World War II, the US Army developed a concept to defeat fast-moving armoured formations using powerfully armed tank destroyers deployed en masse. The M10 was a product of this concept. Based on the M4 Sherman tank chassis and using the M7 gun, developed from an anti-aircraft weapon, the M10 was lightly armed as it was not intended for close-quarter combat. Production ran from September to December 1942, with nearly 5000 being produced. The concept of separate tank destroyer battalions was soon proved ineffective, and thus most M10s were used more as assault forces. The M10 continued in service until the end of the war, but its large and bulky nature and the diminishing effect of its gun reduced its usefulness.

SPECIFICATIONS

COUNTRY OF ORIGIN: United States
CREW: 5
WEIGHT: 29,937kg (65,999lb)
DIMENSIONS: length 6.83m (22ft 5in); width 3.05m (10ft); height 2.57m (8ft 5in)
RANGE: 322km (200 miles)
ARMOUR: 12–37mm (0.47–1.46in)
ARMAMENT: 1 x 76.2mm (3in) M7 gun; 1 x 12.7mm (0.5in) Browning machine gun
POWERPLANT: 2 x General Motors 6-cylinder diesel engines each developing 375hp (276.6kW)
PERFORMANCE: maximum road speed 51km/h (32mph); fording 0.91m (2ft 11in); vertical obstacle 0.46m (1ft 6in); trench 2.26m (7ft 5in)

Marder II

By 1941, the PzKpfw II was becoming obsolete. However, the production line was still in operation, so in order not to waste resources, the decision was taken to convert the chassis to a tank destroyer to tackle the large numbers of Soviet tanks on the Eastern Front. The standard Pak 40 anti-tank gun was mounted on the PzKpfw II's chassis. The combination of firepower and mobility worked well and the Marder II as it was known remained in production until 1944, with 1217 being made. The Marder II saw action in all theatres, particularly on the Eastern front, where some were later equipped with infrared systems for night-fighting. The Marder II proved an effective and versatile weapon and was the most widely used German self-propelled gun of World War II.

SPECIFICATIONS

COUNTRY OF ORIGIN: Germany
CREW: 3 or 4
WEIGHT: 11,000kg (24,250lb)
DIMENSIONS: length 6.36m (20ft 10in); width 2.28m (7ft 6in); height 2.20m (7ft 3in)
RANGE: 190km (118 miles)
ARMOUR: 10mm (0.39in)
ARMAMENT: 1 x 7.5cm (2.95in) Pak 40/2 gun; 1 x 7.92mm (0.31in) MG34 machine gun
POWERPLANT: 1 x Maybach HL 62 petrol engine developing 140hp (104.4kW)
PERFORMANCE: maximum road speed 40km/h (24.8mph); fording 0.9m (2ft 11in); vertical obstacle 0.42m (1ft 4in); trench 1.8m (5ft 11in)

Jagdpanzer IV

Experience during 1942 suggested that the Sturmgeschütz vehicles would have to be upgunned if their role as tank destroyers was to continue. The armament of the Panther was selected, and while modifications were made to the Sturmgeschütz III to allow for this upgrade, the Panther gun was fitted to the chassis of the PzKpfw IV. Known as the Jagdpanzer IV, the first production models appeared in 1943. With a low silhouette and well-protected hull, the Jagdpanzer IV soon proved popular with crews, especially as the armament proved sufficient to knock out almost any enemy tank encountered. Under Hitler's instructions, some were later fitted with the more powerful L/70 gun, but the extra weight resulted in less mobility. A total of 1139 were produced between December 1943 and March 1945.

SPECIFICATIONS

COUNTRY OF ORIGIN: Germany
CREW: 4
WEIGHT: 25,800kg (56,879lb)
DIMENSIONS: length 8.58m (28ft 2in); width 2.93m (9ft 7in); height 1.96m (6ft 5in)
RANGE: 214km (133 miles)
ARMOUR: 11–80mm (0.43–3.14in)
ARMAMENT: 1 x 7.5cm (2.95in) Pak 39 gun; two 7.92mm (0.31in) MG34 machine guns
POWERPLANT: 1 x Maybach HL 120 petrol engine developing 265hp (197.6kW)
PERFORMANCE: maximum road speed 35km/h (22mph); fording 1.2m (3ft 11in); vertical obstacle 0.6m (1ft 11in); trench 2.3m (7ft 6in)

Nashorn

In an effort to get sizeable numbers of tank destroyers into service on the Eastern Front, the Germans embarked on a series of hurried improvisations. A special weapon-carrier vehicle based on the PzKpfw IV chassis was adapted to take the 8.8cm (3.46in) Pak 43 gun. The first of these so-called Nashorns entered service in 1943. The Nashorn was a high vehicle which was difficult to conceal, a problem increased by poor armour with only the driver being fully protected. It was therefore used as a long-range weapon, in contrast to most other tank destroyers. Some 433 were built before production ceased in 1944. The powerful gun made the Nashorn a potent battlefield weapon, but it was too bulky for its prescribed role and only the lack of anything better kept it in production in Germany.

SPECIFICATIONS

COUNTRY OF ORIGIN: Germany
CREW: 5
WEIGHT: 24,400kg (53,792lb)
DIMENSIONS: length 8.44m (27ft 8in); width 2.86m (9ft 5in); height 2.65m (8ft 8in)
RANGE: 210km (131 miles)
ARMOUR: 10–30mm (0.39–1.18in)
ARMAMENT: 1 x 8.8cm (3.46in) Pak 43 gun; 1 x 7.92mm (0.31in) MG34 machine gun
POWERPLANT: 1 x Maybach HL 120 petrol engine developing 265hp (197.6kW)
PERFORMANCE: maximum road speed 40km/h (24.8mph); fording 0.8m (2ft 8in); vertical obstacle 0.6m (24in); trench 2.3m (7ft 7in)

Hetzer

Most tank destroyer conversions of existing tank chassis were rather cumbersome and lacked finesse in design. In contrast, the various Sturmgeschütz artillery vehicles had proved very effective tank killers, so it was decided to produce a light tank destroyer along the lines of a Sturmgeschütz. Based on the PzKpfw 38(t) chassis, the new Hetzer was put into production in 1943. Small, well-protected, with good mobility and able to knock out all but the heaviest tanks, the Hetzer was a tremendous success. By the time the factories were overrun in May 1944, 1577 had been built, including flame-thrower and recovery versions. The Czech Army took over production of the Hetzer after World War II and exports were still in service with the Swiss in the 1970s.

SPECIFICATIONS

COUNTRY OF ORIGIN: Germany
CREW: 4
WEIGHT: 14,500kg (31,967lb)
DIMENSIONS: length 6.20m (20ft 4in); width 2.50m (8ft 2in); height 2.10m (6ft 10in)
RANGE: 250km (155 miles)
ARMOUR: 10–60mm (0.39–2.36in)
ARMAMENT: 1 x 7.5cm (2.95in) Pak 39 gun; 1 x 7.92mm (0.31in) MG34 machine gun
POWERPLANT: one Praga AC/2800 petrol engine developing 150-160hp (111.9-119.3kW)
PERFORMANCE: maximum road speed 39km/h (24.2mph); fording 0.9m (2ft 11in); vertical obstacle 0.65m (2ft 1in); trench 1.3m (4ft 3in)

Renault FT-17

The FT-17 was one of the most successful of all World War I tanks. It was the first of the classic tank design with features mounted directly onto the hull and a turret with a 360-degree traverse. They were ordered in large numbers (over 3000 during World War I) and needed to be, for they had been designed with little thought for maintenance and repair and as a result were often out of action. A self-propelled gun version and a radio-equipped version were among variants produced. In action, they were used en masse. For example, 480 being used in a counter-attack near Soissons in July 1918 alone. They remained in service right up until 1944, when the Germans used captured FT-17s for street-fighting in Paris. By this time, of course, they were hopelessly out of date.

SPECIFICATIONS
COUNTRY OF ORIGIN: France
CREW: 2
WEIGHT: 6600kg (14,550lb)
DIMENSIONS: length (with tail) 5.0m (16ft 5in); width 1.71m (5ft 7.33in); height 2.133m (7ft in)
RANGE: 35.4km (22 miles)
ARMOUR: 16mm (0.63in)
ARMAMENT: 1 x 37mm (1.46in) gun or one machine gun
POWERPLANT: 1 x 35hp (26kW) Renault 4-cylinder petrol engine
PERFORMANCE: maximum road speed 7.7km/h (4.8mph)

Whippet Mk A

The World War I Medium Tank Mk A was designed not so much for crossing obstacles as for exploiting breakthroughs brought about by heavier tanks. The emphasis was thus on speed and mobility. Designed by William Tritton, the Mk A was soon nicknamed 'Whippet'. The prototype was powered by London bus engines and was ready in February 1917, but it was not until late 1917 that the first production models appeared. The Whippet first saw combat in March 1918, being used initially to plug gaps in the line. Its worth was proved in counter-attacks, making deep forays behind the lines and creating havoc in the German rear areas. After the war, the Mk A saw service in Ireland and a number were exported to Japan in the 1920s.

SPECIFICATIONS

COUNTRY OF ORIGIN: United Kingdom
CREW: 3 or 4
WEIGHT: 14,300kg (31,460lb)
DIMENSIONS: length 6.10m (20ft); width 2.62m (8ft 7in); height 2.74m (9ft)
RANGE: 257km (160 miles)
ARMOUR: 5–14mm (0.2–0.55in)
ARMAMENT: 2 x Hotchkiss machine guns
POWERPLANT: 2 x 45hp (33.6kW) Tylor 4-cylinder petrol engines
PERFORMANCE: maximum road speed 13.4km/h (8.3mph)

T-28

Inspired by British and German tank designs, the T-28 medium tank had a centrally mounted main turret and two auxiliary machine gun turrets in front. The vehicle's suspension was directly copied from the British Vickers vehicle, and though the prototype was armed with a 45mm (1.77in) main gun, production models were equipped with the more powerful 76.2mm (3in) low-velocity gun. There were a number of different models and variants, some of which were produced as a result of combat experience. The T-28C, for example, was given additional armour on the hull front and turret as a result of the Red Army's unhappy time in the Russo-Finnish War. An interesting variant was the T-28(V), a commander's tank fitted with a radio which had a frame aerial round the turret.

SPECIFICATIONS

COUNTRY OF ORIGIN: Soviet Union/Russia
CREW: 6
WEIGHT: 28,509kg (62,851lb)
DIMENSIONS: length 7.44m (24ft 5in); width 2.81m (9ft 3in); height 2.82m (9ft 3in)
RANGE: 220km (137 miles)
ARMOUR: 10–80mm (0.39–3.15in)
ARMAMENT: 1 x 76.2mm (3in) gun; 3 x 7.62mm (0.3in) machine guns
POWERPLANT: 1 x M-17 V-12 petrol engine developing 500hp (373kW)
PERFORMANCE: maximum road speed 37km/h (23mph); fording not known; vertical obstacle 1.04m (3ft 5in); trench 2.90m (9ft 6in)

Type 95 Light Tank

The Type 95, known as the KE-GO, was developed in the early 1930s to meet the requirements of the Japanese Army at that time. When production ceased in 1943, over 1100 had been built. The major drawback of the vehicle was that the commander had to operate the gun in addition to his normal duties, which impeded combat effectiveness. While this was acceptable when faced with infantry in Manchuria, it proved disastrous when up against American armour in the later years of the war. Despite later upgunning, the tank's poor armour and lack of firepower ensured that it was wholly inadequate. The Type 95 also served as the basis for the Type 2 KA-MI amphibious tank which was widely used in the early Pacific campaigns of World War II.

SPECIFICATIONS

COUNTRY OF ORIGIN: Japan
CREW: 4
WEIGHT: 7400kg (16,280lb)
DIMENSIONS: length 4.38m (14ft 4in); width 2.06m (6ft 9in); height 2.18m (7ft 2in)
RANGE: 250km (155 miles)
ARMOUR: 6–14mm (0.25–0.6in)
ARMAMENT: 1 x 37mm (1.46in) gun; 2 x 7.7mm (0.3in) machine guns
POWERPLANT: 1 x Mitsubishi NVD 6120 6-cylinder air-cooled diesel engine developing 120hp (89kW)
PERFORMANCE: maximum road speed 45km/h (28mph); fording 1m (3ft 3in); vertical obstacle 0.81m (2ft 8in); trench 2m (6ft 7in)

Panzer I

The Panzer I was the first German tank to go into mass production, with nearly 600 having being ordered by July 1934. Three separate companies were engaged to build the tank (deliberately to spread experience of tank manufacture as widely as possible) and over 800 had been produced by June 1936, when production ceased. To avoid being seen to break the Treaty of Versailles, which prohibited the Germans from building tanks, the design was disguised as an 'agricultural tractor'. The Panzer I Ausf A was found in varying numbers in all panzer units and served extensively during the early campaigns of World War II. However, its limitations in armour and armament were soon evident, and it had been withdrawn from frontline service by 1941.

SPECIFICATIONS

COUNTRY OF ORIGIN: Germany
CREW: 2
WEIGHT: 5500kg (12,125lb)
DIMENSIONS: length 4.02m (13ft 2in); width 2.06m (6ft 9in); height 1.72m (5ft 7in)
RANGE: 145km (81 miles)
ARMOUR: 6–13mm (0.2–0.5in)
ARMAMENT: 2 x 7.92mm (0.31in) MG13 machine guns
POWERPLANT: 1 x Krupp M305 petrol engine developing 60hp (45kW)
PERFORMANCE: maximum road speed 37 km/h (21mph); fording 0.85m (2ft 10in); vertical obstacle 0.42m (1ft 5in); trench 1.75m (5ft 9in)

Panzer II

The first production model PzKpfw II Ausf A appeared in 1935, having been designated as a tractor since German rearmament was hindered by the restrictions of the Treaty of Versailles. The initial tanks were a collaboration between the firms of MAN and Daimler-Benz. The Ausf B, C, D, E, and F versions were built during the years up to 1941, the main improvements being in the thickness of the armour. The tank formed the backbone of the invasions of Poland and France, with around 1000 seeing service. By the time of the invasion of the Soviet Union in 1941, the tank was obsolete but was used as the basis for the Luchs reconnaissance tank. Other variants included an amphibious version designed for the invasion of Britain and the Flammpanzer II flame-throwing tank.

SPECIFICATIONS

COUNTRY OF ORIGIN: Germany
CREW: 3
WEIGHT: 10,000 kg (22,046lb)
DIMENSIONS: length 4.64m (15ft 3in); width 2.30m (7ft 7in); height 2.02m (6ft 8in)
RANGE: 200km (124 miles)
ARMOUR: (Ausf F version) 20–35mm (0.8–1.38in)
ARMAMENT: 1 x 20mm (0.79in) cannon; 1 x 7.92mm (0.31in) machine gun
POWERPLANT: 1 x Maybach 6-cylinder petrol engine developing 140hp (104kW)
PERFORMANCE: maximum road speed 55km/h (34mph); fording 0.85m (2ft 10in); vertical obstacle 0.42m (1ft 5in); trench 1.75m (5ft 9in)

Renault R-35

The Renault R-35 was designed in the mid-1930s to replace the ageing World War I-vintage Renault FT-17. By 1940, some 1600 had been built and it was the most numerous French tank in service, even though it never managed to fulfil its role as the FT-17's replacement. An adequate vehicle, it was no match for German panzers, particularly as it was deployed piecemeal against their massed formations. The gun was unable to penetrate even light German armour and many were abandoned during the French retreat in May 1940. The Germans used the R-35 as a garrison and training tank and adapted many for use as artillery tractors, ammunition carriers and self-propelled artillery carriages. For the latter, the turrets were removed and used for coastal defences.

SPECIFICATIONS

COUNTRY OF ORIGIN: France
CREW: 2
WEIGHT: 10,000kg (22,046lb)
DIMENSIONS: length 4.20m (13ft 9in); width 1.85m (6ft 1in); height 2.37m (7ft 9in)
RANGE: 140km (87 miles)
ARMOUR: 40mm (1.57in)
ARMAMENT: 1 x 37mm (1.46in) gun; one coaxial 7.5mm (0.29in) machine gun
POWERPLANT: 1 x Renault 4-cylinder petrol engine developing 82hp (61kW)
PERFORMANCE: maximum road speed 20km/h (12.4mph); fording 0.80m (2ft 7in); vertical obstacle 0.50m (1ft 8in); trench 1.60m (5ft 3in)

Fiat-Ansaldo L3/35Lf

In 1929, the Italian Army purchased 25 British Carden Lloyd Mk VI tankettes for use in mountainous terrain. Subsequently, Fiat-Ansaldo produced their own version, the Carro Veloce 29 (CV 29), which began an entire series of Italian tankettes. In 1938, the variants numbered CV 3/33 and 3/35 were redesignated as L3. The most basic L3s were armed with a Breda 13.2mm (0.52in) machine gun, but the L3/35Lf flame-thrower version became the most prevalent of the L3 series. The flamethrower barrel extended from the left of the barbette, and the L3/35Lf had its own internal flame-liquid tank. L3s served extensively in North Africa and during the later Italian campaign.

SPECIFICATIONS

COUNTRY OF ORIGIN: Italy
CREW: 2
WEIGHT: 3300kg (7275lb)
DIMENSIONS: length 3.2m (10ft 6in); width 1.42m (4ft 7in); height 1.3m (4ft 3in)
RANGE: 120km (75 miles)
ARMOUR: not available
ARMAMENT: 1 x flame-thrower
POWERPLANT: 1 x Fiat four-cylinder petrol, developing 40hp (30kW)
PERFORMANCE: maximum road speed: 42km/h (26mph)

Somua S-35

The SOMUA S-35 was one of the first tanks used to mechanize the French cavalry in the mid-1930s. It was a very advanced vehicle for its time and many of its features were to become standard for future tank designs, such as cast, rather than rivetted, armour. A radio was fitted as standard and the tank was supplied with a sufficiently powerful main armament to be still in service in German hands on D-Day in June 1944. Production was slow and there were only around 250 in frontline service by the time the Germans invaded in 1940. The major drawback was that the commander was required to operate the gun and the radio as well as his normal duties. Despite this reduced effectiveness, the S-35 was still the best Allied tank in service in 1940 (which says a lot about Allied armoured strength).

SPECIFICATIONS

COUNTRY OF ORIGIN: France
CREW: 3
WEIGHT: 19,500kg (42,900lb)
DIMENSIONS: length 5.38m (17ft 8in); width 2.12m (6ft 11in); height 2.62m (8ft 7in)
RANGE: 230km (143 miles)
ARMOUR: 20–55mm (0.8–2.2in)
ARMAMENT: 1 x 47mm (1.85in) gun; one coaxial 7.5mm (0.29in) machine gun
POWERPLANT: 1 x SOMUA V-8 petrol engine developing 190hp (141.7kW)
PERFORMANCE: maximum road speed 40km/h (24.85mph); fording 1.0m (3ft 3in); vertical obstacle 0.76m (2ft 6in); trench 2.13m (7ft)

Vickers Light Tank Mk VIB

Originally based on the Carden-Loyd tankette of the 1920s, the Vickers light tanks were developed in the 1930s. Mobile and fast across country, the Vickers was widely used in the 1930s for policing the British Empire and in the early years of World War II. However, World War II combat experience proved them to be virtually useless. Their thin armour was easily pierced and their machine-gun armament was utterly inadequate on the battlefield. Lack of equipment forced the British to use them in combat rather than for reconnaissance, as they were designed to be used, and the consequences were disastrous. Attempts to convert them into anti-aircraft tanks failed, although the Germans managed to employ some captured vehicles as anti-tank gun carriers.

SPECIFICATIONS

COUNTRY OF ORIGIN: United Kingdom
CREW: 3
WEIGHT: 4877kg (10,752lb)
DIMENSIONS: length 3.96m (13ft); width 2.08m (6ft 10in); height 2.24m (7ft 6in)
RANGE: 201km (125 miles)
ARMOUR: 10–15mm (0.4–0.6in)
ARMAMENT: 1 x 7.7mm (0.303in)/12.7mm (0.5in) machine gun
POWERPLANT: 1 x Meadows ESTL 6-cylinder petrol engine developing 88hp (66kW)
PERFORMANCE: maximum road speed 51.5km/h (32mph); fording 0.6m (2ft)

Char B1

The first B1s appeared in 1937. Despite its appearance, which was reminiscent of World War I tanks, the Char B1 was a powerful tank for the time and carried a range of advanced design features, such as self-sealing fuel tanks. The crew were seated some way from each other, however, which made internal communication difficult. These crews needed to be highly trained to operate the B1 to full advantage, and such crews were rare in 1940. In addition, the tank's complexities made maintenance difficult and many broke down in combat. Those that entered the fray were really too cumbersome for their powerful armament to have much effect. The Germans later employed captured Char B1s as training tanks or self-propelled artillery carriages.

SPECIFICATIONS

COUNTRY OF ORIGIN: France
CREW: 4
WEIGHT: 31,500kg (69,445lb)
DIMENSIONS: length 6.37m (20ft 11in); width 2.50m (8ft 2in); height 2.79m (9ft 2in)
RANGE: 180km (112 miles)

ARMOUR: 14–65mm (0.6–2.6in)
ARMAMENT: 1 x 75mm (2.95in) gun; one 45mm (1.77in) gun
POWERPLANT: 1 x Renault 6-cylinder petrol engine developing 307hp (229kW)
PERFORMANCE: maximum road speed 28km/h (17.4mph); fording not known; vertical obstacle 0.93m (3ft 1in); trench 2.74m (8ft 11in)

Tetrarch Mk VII

When the prototype of the Tetrarch, known at the time as the Purdah, appeared in 1938, it was received without enthusiasm as it had no outstanding attributes. Like other light tanks, it fared badly in combat in the early years of the war, being poorly armed and armoured and lacking a specified purpose. It was withdrawn quickly, although some were passed on to the Soviet Union (where it was greeted with a similar lack of enthusiasm). However, it was given new life as an airborne tank and the Hamilcar glider was specifically designed to carry it. Fitted with a more powerful armament, the tank landed with British airborne forces on D-Day, but proved no match for enemy armour and its role was later assumed by the American M22 Locust.

SPECIFICATIONS

COUNTRY OF ORIGIN: United Kingdom
CREW: 3
WEIGHT: 7620kg (16,764lb)
DIMENSIONS: length (overall) 4.31m (14ft 2in); length (of hull) 4.12m (13ft 6in); width 2.31m (7ft 7in); height 2.121m (6ft 11in)
RANGE: 224km (140 miles)
ARMOUR: 4–16mm (0.16–0.63in)
ARMAMENT: 1 x 2-pounder gun; 1 x coaxial 7.92mm (0.31in) machine gun
POWERPLANT: 1 x Meadows 12-cylinder petrol engine developing 165hp (123kW)
PERFORMANCE: maximum road speed 64km/h (40mph); maximum cross-country speed 45km/h (28mph); fording 0.91m (3ft); trench 1.524m (5ft)

Hotchkiss H-39

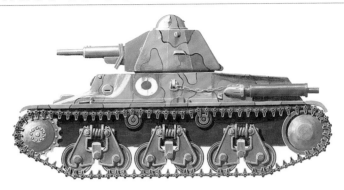

The Hotchkiss H-39 first appeared in 1939, intended for use by French cavalry formations. Despite production problems common to all French tanks in the period before World War II, about 1000 were built. The tank gave a good account of itself in combat during the German invasion of France in 1940, but had too little firepower to compete with enemy armour. In addition, French tactics at the time envisaged tanks being used as infantry support rather than in mass formations, diminishing its effectiveness. After the surrender, the Germans employed the H-39 for occupation duties. Some saw action with the Free French and Vichy French forces in the Middle East, where they were later used by the Israelis, remaining in service until 1956.

SPECIFICATIONS

COUNTRY OF ORIGIN: France
CREW: 2
WEIGHT: 12,100kg (26,676lb)
DIMENSIONS: length 4.22m (13ft 10in); width 1.95m (6ft 5in); height 2.15m (7ft 1in)
RANGE: 120km (74.5 miles)
ARMOUR: 40mm (1.57in)
ARMAMENT: 1 x 37mm (1.47in) gun; one coaxial 7.5mm (0.29in) machine gun
POWERPLANT: 1 x Hotchkiss 6-cylinder petrol engine developing 120hp (89.5kW)
PERFORMANCE: maximum road speed 36km/h (22.3mph); fording 0.85m (2ft 10in); vertical obstacle 0.50m (1ft 8in); trench 1.80m (5ft 11in)

KV-1 Heavy Tank

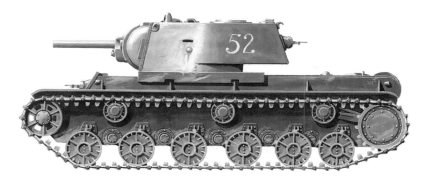

Design on the KV-1 began in 1938, with the intention that it should be the successor to the T-35 heavy tank. The first models were field-tested during the Red Army's disastrous 1940 campaign in Finland. Nevertheless, the KV-1 set the standard for Soviet tank design for several years to come and proved to be a formidable vehicle, being used as an assault tank or to spearhead breakthroughs. However, the tank was not particularly mobile and suffered from automotive problems. In addition, it was uparmoured progressively without any increase in power being allotted, which resulted in poor power-to-weight ratio and performance. The importance of the KV-1 is that it paved the way for later generations of Russian heavy tanks, such as the Josef Stalin.

SPECIFICATIONS

COUNTRY OF ORIGIN: Soviet Union/Russia
CREW: 5
WEIGHT: 43,000kg (94,799lb)
DIMENSIONS: length 6.68m (21ft 11in); width 3.32m (10ft 11in); height 2.71m (8ft 10in)
RANGE: 150km (93 miles)
ARMOUR: 100mm (3.94in)
ARMAMENT: 1 x 76.2mm (3in) gun; four 7.62mm (0.3in) machine guns
POWERPLANT: 1 x V-2K V-12 diesel engine developing 600hp (448kW)
PERFORMANCE: maximum (rarely achieved) road speed 35km/h (21.75mph); fording not known; vertical obstacle 1.20m (3ft 8in); trench 2.59m (8ft 6in)

Matilda Infantry Tank

The Mk I Matilda was developed in response to a 1934 requirement for an infantry tank. Well-armoured for its day, it was a small, simple tank. However, despite being sturdy enough to withstand hits from most German tank guns in the early stages of World War II, it was too poorly armed to be of much use as the war progressed. The Mk II had improved armament and this helped the Matilda to fare reasonably well in combat, particularly in North Africa where it was widely used in the run-up to El Alamein in 1942. Following its replacement in frontline service, the Matilda was used for a variety of specialized roles, such as mine-clearing (the Baron); as a flame-thrower tank (the Frog); and as the basis of a Canal Defence Light for illuminating night operations.

SPECIFICATIONS

COUNTRY OF ORIGIN: United Kingdom
CREW: 4
WEIGHT: 26,926kg (59,237lb)
DIMENSIONS: length 5.613m (18ft 5in); width 2.59m (8ft 6in); height 2.51m (8ft 3in)
RANGE: 257km (160 miles)
ARMOUR: 20–78mm (0.8–3.1in)
ARMAMENT: 1 x 2-pounder gun; 1 x 7.92mm (0.31in) Besa machine gun
POWERPLANT: 2 x Leyland 6-cylinder petrol engines each developing 95hp (71kW) or 2 x AEC diesels each developing 87hp (65kW)
PERFORMANCE: maximum speed 24km/h (15mph); maximum cross-country speed 12.9km/h (8mph); fording 0.91m (2ft 11in); vertical obstacle 0.61m (2ft); trench 2.13m (6ft 11in)

Panzer III

F ollowing a 1935 German Army requirement for a light medium tank design, Daimler-Benz began mass production of the Pzkpfw III in September 1939. The early Ausf A, B and C models saw action in Poland, and in 1940 the Ausf F entered production, with heavier armour and an uprated engine. By the time the final version, the Ausf N, ceased production in August 1943, when the army was fighting in Russia, the tank carried twice as big a gun and weighed twice as much as the original prototype. Variants included an amphibious version, a command vehicle, an armoured recovery vehicle, an observation vehicle and one adapted for desert warfare. In addition, the chassis was used for a number of self-propelled guns right to the end of World War II in 1945.

SPECIFICATIONS

COUNTRY OF ORIGIN: Germany
CREW: 5
WEIGHT: 22,300kg (49,163lb)
DIMENSIONS: length 6.41m (21ft); width 2.95m (9ft 8in); height 2.50m (8ft 2.5in)
RANGE: 175km (109 miles)
ARMOUR: 30mm (1.18in)
ARMAMENT: (Ausf M version) 1 x 75mm (2.95in) L/24 gun; 1 x 7.92mm (0.31in) machine gun
POWERPLANT: 1 x Maybach HL 120 TRM 12-cylinder petrol engine developing 300hp (224kW)
PERFORMANCE: maximum road speed 40km/h (25mph); fording 0.8m (2ft 8in); vertical obstacle 0.6m (1ft 11in); trench 2.59m (8ft 6in)

Panzer IV

The PzKpfw IV was built under a 1934 requirement from the German Army Weapons Department and was later to become the backbone of the Wehrmacht's panzer arm. The tank was in production right throughout the war, with the final version, the Ausf J, appearing in March 1944. In total, nearly 9000 vehicles were built by Krupp, with the basic chassis remaining the same in all models, but with heavier armour and armament being added as requirements changed. Despite the extra weight, the PzKpfw IV retained a good power-to-weight ratio throughout its production life and thus had good mobility. Like the Panzer III, the chassis was used as the basis for various self-propelled guns as well as armoured recovery vehicles and bridge-layers and the Jagdpanzer IV tank destroyer.

SPECIFICATIONS

COUNTRY OF ORIGIN: Germany
CREW: 5
WEIGHT: 25,000kg (55,115lb)
DIMENSIONS: length 7.02m (23ft); width 3.29m (10ft 10in); height 2.68m (8ft 10in)
RANGE: 200km (124 miles)
ARMOUR: 50–60mm (1.97–2.4in)
ARMAMENT: (Ausf H version) 1 x 75mm (2.95in) gun; 2 x 7.92mm (0.31in) MG 34 machine guns
POWERPLANT: 1 x Maybach HL 120 TRM 12-cylinder petrol engine developing 300hp (224kW)
PERFORMANCE: maximum road speed 38km/h (24mph); fording 1.0m (3ft 3in); vertical obstacle 0.6m (1ft 11in); trench 2.20m (7ft 3in)

PzKpfw 38(t)

The Panzerkampfwagen (PzKpfw) – armoured fighting vehicle – 38(t) began life as the Czech-designed LT vz 38, although none had entered service with the Czech Army prior to the German occupation of Czechoslovakia in 1938. More than 1400 were built for the Axis forces between 1939–42. When it became outclassed as a light tank, the type was used widely as a reconnaissance vehicle and the chassis was used as the basis for a large number of vehicles, including the Marder tank destroyer, several self-propelled anti-aircraft guns, a weapons carrier and the Hetzer tank destroyer, which continued in service with the Swiss Army until the late 1960s. During its combat career its armour thickness was steadily increase. For example, the Ausf E version onwards had armour 50mm (2in) thick.

SPECIFICATIONS

COUNTRY OF ORIGIN: Germany
CREW: 4
WEIGHT: 9700kg (21,385lb)
DIMENSIONS: length 4.55m (14ft 11in); width 2.13m (6ft 11in); height 2.311m (7ft 7in)
RANGE: 200km (124 miles)
ARMOUR: 10–25mm (0.4–1in); later increased from Ausf E version onwards to 50mm (2in)
ARMAMENT: 1 x 37.2mm (1.46in) Skoda A7 gun; 2 x 7.92mm (0.31in) machine guns
POWERPLANT: 1 x Praga EPA 6-cylinder water-cooled inline petrol engine developing 150hp (112kW)
PERFORMANCE: maximum road speed 42km/h (26mph); fording 0.9m (2ft 11in); vertical obstacle 0.79m (2ft 7in); trench 1.88m (6ft 2in)

SdKfz 265

The concept of the Command Tank came about following the realization that the leaders of massed Panzer formations would not only have to travel in tanks themselves, but the vehicles would have to carry extra equipment and personnel to assist the commander in his duties. In 1938, the PzKpfw I training tank was converted. The rotating hull was changed to a box superstructure to give more space and allow room for map boards and paperwork (though even then the space was not voluminous). More powerful radios were installed and a signaller added to the crew. Around 200 conversions were made, and the tank first saw action in the Polish Campaign in September 1939, later being used in France and North Africa, before being replaced by conversions of larger tanks.

SPECIFICATIONS

COUNTRY OF ORIGIN: Germany
CREW: 3
WEIGHT: 5800kg (12,787lb)
DIMENSIONS: length 4.45m (14ft 7in); width 2.08m (6ft 10in); height 1.72m (5ft 8in)
RANGE: 290km (180 miles)
ARMOUR: 6–13mm (0.24–0.5in)
ARMAMENT: 1 x 7.92mm (0.31in) machine gun
POWERPLANT: 1 x Maybach NL38TR petrol engine developing 100hp (74.6kW)
PERFORMANCE: maximum road speed 40km/h (25mph); fording 0.85m (2ft 10in); vertical obstacle 0.42m (1ft 5in); trench 1.75m (5ft 9in)

Fiat L6/40

The Fiat L6/40 arose from a 1930s design based on the British Carden-Loyd Mark VI tankette. Intended primarily for export, the first production models arrived in 1939 and a total of 283 were built. At the time of its introduction, the L6/40 was roughly equivalent to the German PzKpfw II, but was never really suitable for frontline service. However, it saw service with reconnaissance and cavalry units in Italy, North Africa and Russia. Variants included a flame-thrower version and a command tank, the latter having extra communications equipment and an open-topped turret. In addition, a number of L6/40s were converted into Semovente L40 self-propelled anti-tank guns. Like most Italian tanks in World War II, it was hopelessly outclassed when it came up against Allied armour.

SPECIFICATIONS

COUNTRY OF ORIGIN: Italy
CREW: 2
WEIGHT: 6800kg (14,991lb)
DIMENSIONS: length 3.78m (12ft 5in); width 1.92m (6ft 4in); height 2.03m (6ft 8in)
RANGE: 200km (124 miles)
ARMOUR: 6–40mm (0.23–1.57in)
ARMAMENT: 1 x Breda Model 35 20mm (0.79in) cannon; one coaxial Breda Model 38 8mm (0.31in) machinegun
POWERPLANT: 1 x SPA 18D 4-cylinder petrol engine developing 70hp (52kW)
PERFORMANCE: maximum road speed 42km/h (26mph); fording 0.8m (2ft 8in); vertical obstacle 0.7m (2ft 4in); trench 1.7m (5ft 7in)

Fiat M13/40

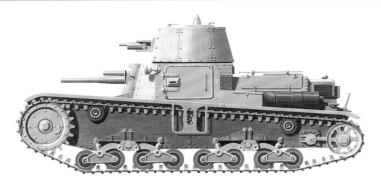

The M13/40 was based on an earlier design, the M11/39, which was not produced in numbers as it was considered already obsolete by the time of its introduction. The M13/40 used the same chassis but had a redesigned hull with better armour. Nearly 800 were produced in total and the tank was widely used in North Africa during Italian attempts to drive British and Commonwealth forces out of the region. In combat the M13/40's shortcomings became very apparent; it was cramped, unreliable and caught fire easily when hit by anti-tank rounds. Many abandoned and captured M13/40s were pressed into service by the British and Australian forces and used to fill a serious shortage of Allied tanks in early 1941. They did not remain in Allied service for long.

SPECIFICATIONS

COUNTRY OF ORIGIN: Italy
CREW: 4
WEIGHT: 14,000kg (30,865lb)
DIMENSIONS: length 4.92m (16ft 2in); width 2.2m (7ft 3in); height 2.38m (7ft 10in)
RANGE: 200km (124 miles)
ARMOUR: 6–42mm (0.24–1.65in)
ARMAMENT: 1 x 47mm (1.85in) gun; 2 x Modello 38 8mm (0.31in) machine guns (one coaxial, one anti-aircraft)
POWERPLANT: 1 x SPA TM40 8-cylinder diesel engine developing 125hp (93kW)
PERFORMANCE: maximum road speed 32km/h (20mph); fording 1.0m (3ft 3in); vertical obstacle 0.8m (2ft 8in); trench 2.1m (6ft 11in)

T-34/76A

The T-34 was an advanced tank for its era, produced in vast numbers to an excellent design, a design borne from two decades of Soviet experimentation and a readiness to embrace the best of foreign ideas. Mass production began in 1940 and its powerful gun and thick armour came as a nasty surprise to the Germans in 1941–42. Finesse was sacrificed for speed of production, but their rough and ready appearance belied their effectiveness. The T-34 was used in every role from recovery vehicle to personnel carrier and reconnaissance and distinguished itself at every turn forcing the Germans back on the defensive. It is no exaggeration to say that the T-34 was the most decisive tank of World War II. The upgunned T34/85 tank introduced in 1944 is still in use with many armies today.

SPECIFICATIONS

COUNTRY OF ORIGIN: Soviet Union/Russia
CREW: 4
WEIGHT: 26,000kg (57,320lb)
DIMENSIONS: length 5.92m (19ft 5in); width 3m (9ft 10in); height 2.44m (8ft)
RANGE: 186km (116 miles)
ARMOUR: 18–60mm (0.71–2.36in)
ARMAMENT: 1 x 76.2mm (3in) gun; 1 x 7.62mm (0.3in) machine guns
POWERPLANT: 1 x V-2-34 V-12 diesel engine developing 500hp (373kW)
PERFORMANCE: maximum road speed 55km/h (34mph); fording 1.37m (4ft 6in); vertical obstacle 0.71m (2ft 4in); trench 2.95m (9ft 8in)

Valentine Mk III

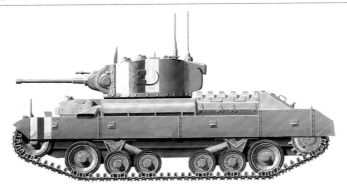

In 1938, Vickers was asked to produce an infantry tank based upon their A10 Cruiser tank. There were initial doubts about the new Valentine's two-man turret, which would limit the possibility of increased armament at a later date, but as war was imminent necessity overcame this caution. Mass production began in 1940 and the Valentine soon proved to be a sturdy, reliable vehicle, if a little slow. Armament was gradually improved as the war progressed, and the Valentine saw service in all theatres. Variants included a mobile bridge, a flame-thrower tank, a mine-clearing tank and a self-propelled gun. Over 8000 Valentines were built before production ceased in 1944, thus making the Valentine one of the most important British tanks in numbers if nothing else.

SPECIFICATIONS

COUNTRY OF ORIGIN: United Kingdom
CREW: 3
WEIGHT: 17,690kg (38,999lb)
DIMENSIONS: length 5.41m (17ft 9in); width 2.63m (8ft 7.5in); height 2.27m (7ft 5in)
RANGE: 145km (90 miles)
ARMOUR: 8–65mm (0.3–2.6in)
ARMAMENT: 1 x 2-pounder gun; 1 x 7.62mm (0.3in) machine gun
POWERPLANT: 1 x AEC diesel developing 131hp (98kW) in Mk III or GMC diesel developing 138hp (103kW) in Mk IV
PERFORMANCE: maximum speed 24km/h (15mph); fording 0.91m (3ft); vertical obstacle 0.84m (2ft 9in); trench 2.2 (7ft 6in)

Canal Defence Light

The basic idea behind the Canal Defence Light (a name chosen to preserve secrecy) was to replace the turret of a tank with a powerful searchlight to illuminate battlefields at night. The idea was first mooted in the mid-1930s, and by late 1939 a turret was ready for production. Initially attached to Matilda II tanks and then Grants, some 300 turrets were ordered. Two British brigades were equipped, one in the United Kingdom and one in North Africa. The light was positioned behind a shutter, which was opened and closed to provide a flickering impression. Somehow, the opportunity to use the CDL never arose and they were confined to providing light for night river crossings and the like. This was probably just as well, for similar Russian experiments proved disastrous in battle.

SPECIFICATIONS

COUNTRY OF ORIGIN: United Kingdom
CREW: 3 or 4
WEIGHT: 26,000kg (57,200lb)
DIMENSIONS: length 5.61m (18ft 5in); width 2.59m (8ft 6in); height 2.51m (8ft 3in)
RANGE: 257km (160 miles)

ARMOUR: 12–38mm (0.47–1.5in)
ARMAMENT: 1 x 7.92mm Besa machine gun
POWERPLANT: 2 x Leyland E148/E149 diesel engines each developing 95hp (70.8kW)
PERFORMANCE: maximum road speed 24km/h (15mph); fording 1.02m (3ft 4in); vertical obstacle 0.61m (2ft); trench 1.91m (6ft 3in)

Churchill Mk IV

The Churchill began life as a 1939 requirement which envisaged a return to trench-warfare, and was thus slow and heavily armoured. The final prototype, however, was a much lighter vehicle than had first been thought of, not unlike a World War I tank in appearance. Rushed into production at a time when invasion seemed imminent, it suffered early reliability problems and was not fully introduced until 1943. Early combat experience during the Dieppe raid in 1942 was disappointing, but the Cromwell proved mobile over rough terrain in North Africa. The tank excelled in its specialized variants, such as the AVRE, the Crocodile flamethrower tank, the bridgelayer and many more. The tank gave excellent service and the final Churchill was not retired until the 1960s.

SPECIFICATIONS

COUNTRY OF ORIGIN: United Kingdom
CREW: 5
WEIGHT: 40,642kg (89,600lb)
DIMENSIONS: length 7.44m (24ft 5in); width 2.44m (8ft); height 3.45m (11ft 4in)
RANGE: 144.8km (90 miles)

ARMOUR: 16–102mm (0.6–4in)
ARMAMENT: 1 x 6-pounder gun; one coaxial 7.62mm (0.3in) machine gun
POWERPLANT: 1 x Bedford twin-six petrol engine developing 350hp (261kW)
PERFORMANCE: maximum speed 20km/h (12.5mph); maximum cross-country speed about 12.8km/h (8mph); fording 1.02m (3ft 4in); vertical obstacle 0.76m (2ft 6in); trench 3.05m (10ft)

Crusader Mk VI

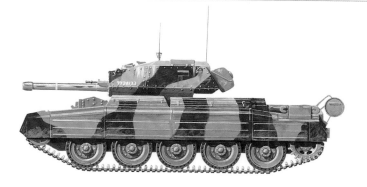

The Crusader's attractive design belied the fact that by the time it first appeared in 1941 it was already outdated. Fast and mobile (their suspension was so tough that theoretical maximum speed was often exceeded), they were thinly armoured and lacked firepower, being no match for their German counterparts. Reliability was also a problem. Even with gradual improvements, the Crusader failed to prove itself in the North African campaigns and was replaced as quickly as possible by the M4 Sherman. Once withdrawn from frontline combat duties, the Crusader was adapted for a variety of roles, such as anti-aircraft tank, recovery vehicle and combat engineer tank with a dozer blade. Many saw service in the last years of the war as artillery tractors, pulling the 17-pounder gun.

SPECIFICATIONS

COUNTRY OF ORIGIN: United Kingdom
CREW: 3
WEIGHT: 20,067kg (44,240lb)
DIMENSIONS: length 5.99m (19ft 8in); width 2.64m (8ft 8in); height 2.24m (7ft 4in)
RANGE: 204km (127 miles)
ARMOUR: 40mm (1.57in)
ARMAMENT: 1 x 2-pounder gun; one coaxial 7.62mm (0.3in) machine gun
POWERPLANT: 1 x Nuffield Liberty Mk III petrol engine developing 340hp (254kW)
PERFORMANCE: maximum road speed 43.4km/h (27mph); maximum cross-country speed 24km/h (15mph); fording 0.99m (3ft 3in); vertical obstacle 0.68m (2ft 3in); trench 2.59 (8ft 6in)

Mörser Karl Ammunition Carrier

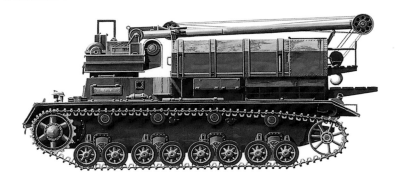

The Karl Ammunition Carrier was designed to supply the massive Mörser Karl Siege Howitzers, the sheer weight of the projectiles – over 2 tonnes (1.96 tons) each – necessitating a new vehicle. The basic tank hull of the PzKpfw IV Ausf D was used, with a platform for the ammunition and a crane added to lift the heavy rounds. The carriers were usually moved by train and assembled near to the point of use, before being driven into position. In 1941, 13 PzKpfw IV Ausf F chassis were converted to ammunition carriers. The Karl Howitzers and Carriers were designed to smash fortifications. They were used rarely in World War II, but did see service during the siege of Sevastopol and during the Battle of Warsaw in 1944, where they were put to devastating use against the defenders.

SPECIFICATIONS

COUNTRY OF ORIGIN: Germany
CREW: 4
WEIGHT: 25,000kg (55,115lb)
DIMENSIONS: length 5.41m (17ft 9in); width 2.88m (9ft 5in); height not recorded
RANGE: 209km (130 miles)
ARMOUR: 60mm (2.4in)
ARMAMENT: none
POWERPLANT: 1 x Maybach HL120 TRM petrol engine developing 300hp (223.7kW)
PERFORMANCE: maximum road speed 39.9km/h (24.8mph); fording 1.0m (3ft 3in); vertical obstacle 0.6m (1ft 11in); trench 2.20m (7ft 3in)

M3 Stuart Light Tank

Having followed the battles of 1940 on the European mainland closely, the American military realized that its main light tank, the M2, was obsolete, and that a more heavily armoured version was required. The result was the M3 which entered full-scale production in 1941, and nearly 6000 were built. Many were passed to the Soviet Red Army and to British forces where they were known as Stuarts. Their reliability and mobility were impressive and they were popular with crews, being used in all theatres of the war. Obsolete as a combat tank by 1944, many were converted to command and reconnaissance vehicles with the turrets removed and extra machine guns added instead. Variants included mine-clearing, flame-throwing and anti-aircraft versions.

SPECIFICATIONS

COUNTRY OF ORIGIN: United States
CREW: 4
WEIGHT: 12,927kg (28,499lb)
DIMENSIONS: length 4.54m (14ft 10in); width 2.24m (7ft 4in); height 2.30m (7ft 6in)
RANGE: 112.6km (70 miles)
ARMOUR: 15–43mm (0.59–1.69in)
ARMAMENT: 1 x 37mm (1.46in) gun; two 7.62mm (0.3in) machine guns
POWERPLANT: 1 x Continental W-970-9A six-cylinder radial petrol engine developing 250hp (186.5kW)
PERFORMANCE: maximum road speed 58km/h (36mph); fording 0.91m (2ft 11in); vertical obstacle 0.61m (2ft); trench 1.83m (6ft)

Ram Mk I Cruiser Tank

At the start of World War II, Canada had no tank units. With no possibility of obtaining tanks from a desperate Britain, the Canadians were forced to build their own. The decision was taken to use the basic components of the American M3, but swap the sponson-mounted main gun for a turret mounting the readily available 40mm (1.57in) gun, with the option of upgunning later. Production began at the end of 1941, but the tank never saw action as by the time it arrived in Europe, the M4 Sherman was being produced in numbers and it was decided to adopt this as the standard for Canadian units. Many Rams had their turrets removed and were used as armoured personnel carriers. The Ram's greatest contribution to the Allied victory was as the basis for the Sexton self-propelled gun.

SPECIFICATIONS

COUNTRY OF ORIGIN: Canada
CREW: 5
WEIGHT: 29,484kg (65,000lb)
DIMENSIONS: length 5.79m (18ft 11in); width 2.89m (9ft 6in); height 2.67m (8ft 9in)
RANGE: 232km (144 miles)
ARMOUR: 25–89mm (1–3.5in)
ARMAMENT: 1 x 2-pounder gun; 1 x coaxial 7.62mm (0.3in) machine guns
POWERPLANT: 1 x Continental R-975 radial petrol engine developing 400hp (298kW)
PERFORMANCE: maximum road speed 40.2km/h (25mph); vertical obstacle 0.61m (2ft); trench 2.26m (7ft 5in)

T-70

The Soviet military had spent a great deal of time and effort in the development of a series of light tanks during the 1930s. The T-70 was the culmination of this effort at the time of the German invasion of Russia in June 1941. Reasonably armoured, the T-70's armament was of limited use against heavier tanks, especially as the commander of the tank had to operate the gun single-handed, thus reducing his combat effectiveness. Its service record was unremarkable, mainly being used for reconnaissance and close infantry support. Over 8000 were produced up to 1943, but despite the numbers, the T-70 was at best only an adequate combat tank. It was certainly better than the tank it superseded, the T-60, but was outgunned by the German panzers in 1941–42.

SPECIFICATIONS

COUNTRY OF ORIGIN: Soviet Union
CREW: 2
WEIGHT: 9367kg (20,608lb)
DIMENSIONS: length 4.29m (14ft 1in); width 2.32m (7ft 7in); height 2.04m (6ft 8in)
RANGE: 360km (224 miles)
ARMOUR: 10–60mm (0.39–2.36in)
ARMAMENT: 1 x 45mm (1.77in) gun; 1 x 7.62mm (0.3in) machine gun
POWERPLANT: 2 x GAZ-202 petrol engines delivering a total of 140hp (104kW)
PERFORMANCE: maximum road speed 45km/h (28mph); fording not known; vertical obstacle 0.70m (2ft 4in); trench 3.12m (10ft 3in)

M3 Lee/Grant Medium Tank

The M3 was developed by the Americans following the realization – based on observation of the armoured battles in France in 1940 – that a more powerful armament would be required than that mounted on the M2 in development at the time. The M3 was shipped to British forces with minor modifications and was known as the General Grant. The Grant proved highly effective against the Afrika Korps in North Africa in its first actions in May 1942, and was popular with the tank crews of hard-pressed British forces. The original version retained by US forces was known as the General Lee. Reliable and hard-wearing, its only drawback was the limited traverse of the hull-mounted main gun. The M3 saw action on all fronts and was widely exported after the war.

SPECIFICATIONS

COUNTRY OF ORIGIN: United States
CREW: 6
WEIGHT: 27,240kg (60,040lb)
DIMENSIONS: length 5.64m (18ft 6in); width 2.72m (8ft 11in); height 3.12m (10ft 3in)
RANGE: 193km (120 miles)
ARMOUR: 12–38mm (0.47–1.5in)
ARMAMENT: 1 x 75mm (2.95in) hull-mounted gun; 1 x 35mm (1.38in) gun on turret; 4 x 7.62mm (0.3in) machine guns
POWERPLANT: 1 x Continental R-975-EC2 radial petrol engine developing 340hp (253.5kW)
PERFORMANCE: maximum road speed 42km/h (26mph); fording 1.02m (3ft 4in); vertical obstacle 0.61m (2ft); trench 1.91m (6ft 3in)

M4A2 Sherman

The M4 Sherman used the same basic hull and suspension as the M3, but mounted the main armament on the gun turret rather than the hull. Easy to build and an excellent fighting platform, it proved to be a war-winner for the Allies. By the time production ceased in 1945, over 40,000 had been built. There were many variants, including engineer tanks, assault tanks, rocket launchers, recovery vehicles and mine-clearers. The British employed the Sherman extensively, notably at El Alamein in 1942. Though outgunned by German tanks and with insufficient armour to compete in the later stages of the war, the sheer numbers produced overwhelmed enemy armoured forces. Its hardiness kept it in service with some South American countries until very recently.

SPECIFICATIONS

COUNTRY OF ORIGIN: United States
CREW: 5
WEIGHT: 31,360kg (69,137lb)
DIMENSIONS: length 5.9m (19ft 4in); width 2.6m (8ft 7in); height 2.74m (9ft)
RANGE: 161km (100 miles)
ARMOUR: 15–76mm (0.59–2.99in)
ARMAMENT: 1 x 75mm (2.95in) gun; one coaxial 7.62mm (0.3in) machine gun; 12.7mm (0.5in) anti-aircraft gun on turret
POWERPLANT: twin General Motors 6-71 diesel engines developing 500hp (373kW)
PERFORMANCE: maximum road speed 46.4km/h (29mph); fording 0.9m (3ft); vertical obstacle 0.61m (2ft); trench 2.26m (7ft 5in)

M4A3 Sherman

The M4A3 was one of the most developed of all the Sherman variants used during World War II. It differed from the M4A2 mainly in the design of its turret and suspension (using a more effective horizontal volute spring system) and in its armament, employing the larger and more powerful 76mm (2.99in) gun as well as having thicker armour. This particular model was the production type most favoured by the US Army. Ford built 1690 A3s between June 1942 and September 1943, before ceasing tank production. Manufacture was then taken over by Grand Blanc from February 1944. Improved features included a vision cupola for the commander, a loader's hatch and so-called 'wet stowage' for the ammunition. In addition, its petrol engine was specifically developed for the vehicle.

SPECIFICATIONS

COUNTRY OF ORIGIN: United States
CREW: 5
WEIGHT: 32,284kg (71,024lb)
DIMENSIONS: length (with gun) 7.52m (24ft 8in) (over hull) 6.27m (20ft 7in); width 2.68m (8ft 10in); height 3.43m (11ft 3in)
RANGE: 161km (100 miles)
ARMOUR: 15–100mm (0.59–3.94in)
ARMAMENT: 1 x 76mm (2.99in) gun; 1 x 7.62mm (0.3in) coaxial machine gun
POWERPLANT: 1 x Ford GAA V-8 petrol engine developing 400 or 500hp (335.6 or 373kW)
PERFORMANCE: maximum road speed 47km/h (29mph); fording 0.91m (3ft); vertical obstacle 0.61m (2ft); trench 2.26m (7ft 5in)

Panzer VI Tiger I

The Tiger heavy tank was produced by Henschel based on a 1941 design and entered production in August 1942. A total of 1350 were built before production ceased in August 1944 and the type was replaced by the King Tiger. There were three main variants: a command tank, a recovery vehicle fitted with a winch and the Sturmtiger, which was fitted with a rocket launcher. The Tiger was an excellent tank, but complicated and therefore difficult to produce in large numbers and maintain. The overlapping wheel suspension had a tendency to clog with mud and stones, which, if it froze in cold conditions such as during the Russian winter, could immobilize the vehicle. It first saw action against the British in Tunisia in 1942 and thereafter appeared on all fronts.

SPECIFICATIONS

COUNTRY OF ORIGIN: Germany
CREW: 5
WEIGHT: 55,000kg (121,254lb)
DIMENSIONS: length 8.24m (27ft); width 3.73m (12ft 3in); height 2.86m (9ft 3in)
RANGE: 100km (62miles)
ARMOUR: 25–100mm (1–3.94in)
ARMAMENT: 1 x 88mm (3.46in) KwK 36 gun; 1 x 7.92mm (0.31in) coaxial MG34 machine gun
POWERPLANT: 1 x Maybach HL 230 P45 12-cylinder petrol engine developing 700hp (522kW)
PERFORMANCE: maximum road speed 38km/h (24mph); fording 1.20m (3ft 11in); vertical obstacle 0.79m (2ft 7in); trench 1.8m (5ft 11in)

Panzer V Panther

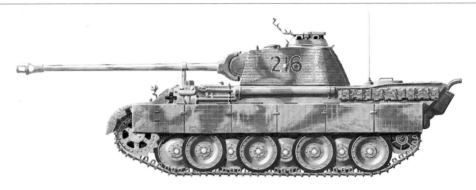

The Panther is widely considered to be one of the best tanks of World War II. Designed to combat the Soviet T-34 tanks which were outclassing the PzKpfw IV on the Eastern Front in early 1942, the Panther fulfilled the requirement for a tank with a powerful gun, good mobility and good protection. MAN completed the first production models in September 1942. The early versions suffered from mechanical problems, particularly at the Battle of Kursk in July 1943, borne from a lack of proper testing. However, once the problems were ironed out, the Panther saw action in all theatres and proved to be very effective. Over 4500 were built up to early 1945, and they continued to see service with the French Army in the immediate post-war period.

SPECIFICATIONS

COUNTRY OF ORIGIN: Germany
CREW: 4
WEIGHT: 45,500kg (100,310lb)
DIMENSIONS: length 8.86m (29ft 1in); width 3.43m (11ft 3in); height 3.10m (10ft 2in)
RANGE: 177km (110miles)
ARMOUR: 30–110mm (1.2–4.3in)
ARMAMENT: 1 x 75mm (2.95in) gun; 3 x 7.92mm (0.31in) MG34 machine guns (1 x coaxial, 1 x anti-aircraft, 1 x on hull front)
POWERPLANT: 1 x Maybach HL 230 12-cylinder diesel developing 700hp (522kW)
PERFORMANCE: maximum road speed 46km/h (29mph); fording 1.70m (5ft 7in); vertical obstacle 0.91m (2ft 11in); trench 1.91m (6ft 3in)

Cromwell Mk IV

The Cromwell was produced in response to a requirement for a more heavily armed and armoured tank to replace the Crusader. The first Cromwells appeared in 1943 armed with a 6-pounder gun. However, it was realized that this would be inadequate and the tanks were soon being equipped with heavier weaponry, which gave some parity with contemporary German tanks. That said, most units were equipped with the M4 Sherman, but the Cromwell gave valuable service as a training tank in the run-up to D-Day and was used for many other roles, such as mobile observation posts and armoured recovery vehicles. Although not quite equal to German tanks, the Cromwell was at least better than previous British efforts and fared reasonably well in combat.

SPECIFICATIONS

COUNTRY OF ORIGIN: United Kingdom
CREW: 5
WEIGHT: 27,942kg (61,602lb)
DIMENSIONS: length 6.42m (21ft 1in); width 3.05m (10ft); height 2.51m (8ft 3in)
RANGE: 278km (173 miles)

ARMOUR: 8–76mm (0.3–3in)
ARMAMENT: 1 x 75mm (2.95in) gun; one coaxial 7.62mm (0.3in) machine gun
POWERPLANT: 1 x Rolls-Royce Meteor V-12 petrol engine developing 570hp (425kW)
PERFORMANCE: maximum speed 61km/h (38mph); fording 1.22m (4ft); vertical obstacle 0.92m (2ft 11in); trench 2.28 (7ft 6in)

Cromwell VI CS

The Cromwell CS (Close Support) variants were identical to the equivalent marks of 'standard' Cromwells except that they were armed with the 95mm (3.7in) CS Howitzer, which originated in late 1941 as a replacement for the unpopular 76mm (3in) CS Howitzer. At the time, this made sense because, until 1943, at least, British tanks were armed with 2-pounder and 6-pounder guns that had a poor performance when firing HE. The new howitzer fired smoke rounds, an 11.34kg (25lb) HE shell to a maximum range of 54.8km (34 miles) and a HEAT round capable of penetrating 100mm (3.94in) of armour. By the time of the Normandy campaign, its value was questionable, as the vast majority of Cromwells in theatre were armed with 75mm (2.95in) guns with adequate HE performance for most tasks. Despite this, Cromwell CS tanks remained in frontline service until well after the end of the war.

SPECIFICATIONS

COUNTRY OF ORIGIN: United Kingom
CREW: 5
WEIGHT: 27,940kg (61,596lb)
LENGTH: 6.35m (20ft 10in)
WIDTH: 2.9m (9ft 6in)
HEIGHT: 2.49m (8ft 2in)
ENGINE: 600hp (450kW) Rolls-Royce Meteor V12 petrol
SPEED: 52km/h (32mph)
RANGE: 278km (173 miles)
ARMAMENT: 1 x 95mm (3.7in) Ordnance QF 95mm (3.74in) Howitzer, plus 2 x 7.92mm (0.31in) Besa machine guns (1 coaxial and 1 ball-mounted in hull front)

Panzer VI Tiger II

The Henschel design for the Tiger II (King Tiger) was completed in October 1943. Early production models carried a turret designed by Porsche, but after the first 50 models had been built, the tanks were wholly produced by Henschel. The tank was similar to the Panther and used the same engine, although its heavier armour, impenetrable to most Allied weapons, resulted in a lower power-to-weight ratio and consequent loss of speed and mobility. The main problem with the Tiger II was unreliability. Many were abandoned by their crews when they broke down or ran out of fuel, as their bulk made them difficult to move or conceal. The Tiger II first saw combat on the Eastern Front in May 1944 and in the battles in Normandy in the autumn of that year.

SPECIFICATIONS

COUNTRY OF ORIGIN: Germany
CREW: 5
WEIGHT: 69,700kg (153,340lb)
DIMENSIONS: length 10.26m (33ft 8in); width 3.75m (12ft 4in); height 3.09m (10ft 2in)
RANGE: 110km (68miles)
ARMOUR: 100–150mm (3.94–5.9in)
ARMAMENT: 1 x 88mm (3.46in) KwK 43 gun; 2 x 7.92mm (0.31in) MG34 machine guns (one coaxial, one on hull front)
POWERPLANT: 1 x Maybach HL 230 P30 12-cylinder petrol developing 700hp (522kW)
PERFORMANCE: maximum road speed 38km/h (24mph); fording 1.60m (5ft 3in); vertical obstacle 0.85m (2ft 10in); trench 2.5m (8ft 2in)

M24 Chaffee

By 1942, it was evident that the 37mm gun was inadequate for the needs of America's light tanks and, indeed, as a main armament of any tank. Attempts to install larger weapons in M5 tanks failed and so a new tank was designed by Cadillac, the first being ready by late 1943. Known as the Chaffee, the M24 entered full service with the US Army in late 1944, too late in the war to make a big impression. It was in Korea that the M24 realized its full combat value, with the agility for reconnaissance, but well-armed for battle. Its biggest contribution was in its concept. It was designed to be part of a combat family of vehicles, all using the same chassis, including self-propelled guns and anti-aircraft tanks. The tank continues to see service with some nations to this day.

SPECIFICATIONS

COUNTRY OF ORIGIN: United States
CREW: 5
WEIGHT: 18,370kg (40,498lb)
DIMENSIONS: length 5.49m (18ft); width 2.95m (9ft 8in); height 2.48m (8ft 2in)
RANGE: 161km (100 miles)
ARMOUR: 12–38mm (0.47–1.5in)
ARMAMENT: 1 x 75mm (2.95in) gun; 2 x 7.62mm (0.3in) machine guns; one 12.7mm (0.5in) gun on turret; one 51mm (2in) smoke mortar
POWERPLANT: 2 x Cadillac Model 44T24 V-8 petrol engines developing 110hp (82kW) each
PERFORMANCE: maximum road speed 56km/h (35mph); fording 1.02m (3ft 4in); vertical obstacle 0.91m (3ft); trench 2.44m (8ft)

Humber Snipe

The Humber Snipe was one of several utility vehicles which entered World War II service with the British Army (others included the Morris Commercial PU and the Ford WOC1). It was based on Humber's civilian vehicle, the Snipe sedan, directly utilizing the chassis, hood and radiator grille. To 'militarize' the vehicle, the bumpers were strengthened, storage boxes were added and a simple tarpaulin cover shielded the driver and passenger. Over 250,000 served British forces in World War II and many variants were produced. The 'General Service' version had seats in the rear area for troop transport or stretchers for medical evacuation. A communications vehicle designated FFW ('Fitted for Wireless') provided mobile radio facilities.

SPECIFICATIONS

COUNTRY OF ORIGIN: United Kingdom
CREW: 4 or 5
WEIGHT: 2170kg (4784lb)
DIMENSIONS: length 4.29m (14ft 1in); width 1.88m (6ft 2in); height 1.89m (6ft 2in)
RANGE: 500km (311 miles)
ARMOUR: none
ARMAMENT: none
POWERPLANT: 1 x Humber 6-cylinder petrol, developing 86hp (64kW)
PERFORMANCE: maximum road speed: 75km/h (46mph)

Opel Blitz

The Opel Blitz was one of the most successful products of an attempt by the Germans to standardize their vehicle fleet (100 different vehicles were in service by the late 1930s, leading to massive logistical difficulties). The Blitz had a steel cab and wooden body and was used in many roles, from field ambulance to mobile workshop to command vehicle. To improve cross-country performance, the vehicle was given four-wheel drive, these vehicles being designated 'Allrad'. They were used in all theatres of the war, with later models being constructed of pressed card to conserve steel. Production lasted until 1944, when Allied bombing and ground advances overtook the factories. The Blitz was well built, but suffered from being too complicated for reliability in rugged conditions.

SPECIFICATIONS

COUNTRY OF ORIGIN: Germany
CREW: 1
WEIGHT: 3290kg (7253lb)
DIMENSIONS: length 6.02m (19ft 9in); width 2.26m (7ft 5.2in); height 2.17m (7ft 1in)
RANGE: 410km (256 miles)
ARMOUR: none
ARMAMENT: none
POWERPLANT: 1 x Opel 6-cylinder petrol engine developing 73.5hp (54.8kW)
PERFORMANCE: maximum road speed 80km/h (50mph); fording 0.5m (1ft 7in)

ZiS-5

The ZiS-5 had its origins in the reformed Automobil Moscow Obshchestvo (AMO) company in 1931. AMO built a range of trucks between 1931 and 1933, at which point the company was renamed Zavod imeni Stalina (ZiS). The AMO trucks were relabelled and, on 1 October 1933, production of the ZiS-5 officially began. It became one of the Russian Army's most prolific vehicles. Nearly one million were produced between 1933 and the mid-1950s. Its wartime service was crucial to Red Army logistics. Wartime vehicles can be spotted by austerity features, such as wooden doors and seats, the absence of bumpers and a fitting of only the left headlight. Production of the ZiS-5 ceased in 1958.

SPECIFICATIONS

COUNTRY OF ORIGIN: Soviet Union/Russia
CREW: 2
WEIGHT: 3100kg (6800lb)
DIMENSIONS: length 6.06m (19ft 10in); width 2.24m (7ft 4in); height 2.16m (7ft 1in)
RANGE: not available
ARMOUR: none
ARMAMENT: none
POWERPLANT: 1 x ZiS-5 6-cylinder petrol, developing 72hp (54kW)
PERFORMANCE: maximum road speed: 65km/h (40mph); fording: 0.6m (2ft)

GAZ-AAA

The GAZ-AAA was one of the earlier offerings from the GAZ company. Production of the vehicle ran between 1933 and 1942. Like many Russian wartime trucks, the 1942 version has radically simplified bodywork – there are no bumpers, the wings and cabin have simplified lines, and there is only one headlight. Though the GAZ-AAA never reached the production figures of the ZiS-5 (qv), 37,373 were made in total. It was a 6 x 4 with a 2500kg (5516lb) payload capacity out of a total loaded weight of 4975kg (10,968lb). The gearbox consisted of eight forward gears and two reverse gears, and it could achieve a maximum road speed of 65km/h (40mph). The chassis of the GAZ-AAA was used to produce the BA-10 armoured car.

SPECIFICATIONS

COUNTRY OF ORIGIN: Soviet Union/Russia
CREW: 2
WEIGHT: 2475kg (5457lb)
DIMENSIONS: length 5.34m (17ft 6in); width 2.04m (6ft 8in); height 1.97m (6ft 5in)
RANGE: not available
ARMOUR: none
ARMAMENT: none
POWERPLANT: 1 x GAZ-M1 4-cylinder petrol, developing 50hp (37kW)
PERFORMANCE: maximum road speed: 65km/h (40mph)

Fiat/Spa 35 Dovunque

The Italian Army in World War II was heavily reliant on trucks of somewhat dated design. Prior to World War II, though, some measure of standardization had been achieved, with Fiat supplying the bulk of the vehicles. Dovunque means literally 'go anywhere', and the truck had adequate cross-country capability, being one of a range of Fiat and other Italian vehicles which saw extensive service, particularly in North Africa. The fact that most needed to be hand-crank started belied their effective performance. The Germans appropriated large numbers of Italian trucks for service in all theatres, and British troops valued captured Italian trucks highly because the vehicles did not rely on a carburettor, which tended to clog up in the dusty desert conditions.

SPECIFICATIONS

COUNTRY OF ORIGIN: Italy
CREW: 1
WEIGHT: 1615kg (3553lb)
DIMENSIONS: length 3.80m (12ft 5in); width 1.30m (4ft 3in); height 2.15m (7ft 1in)
RANGE: 250km (155 miles)
ARMOUR: none
ARMAMENT: none
POWERPLANT: 1 x OM Autocarretta 32 4-cylinder petrol engine developing 21hp (15.7kW)
PERFORMANCE: maximum road speed 63km/h (40mph); fording 0.5m (1ft 7in)

GMC 6 x 6

The GMC 6 x 6 was built for the US Army as part of a standardization programme, begun in 1939, which allowed for only two of each type of vehicle to be considered, and emphasized commonality of parts and accessories wherever possible. Known as 'Jimmies', the vehicles were supplied to Britain under the Lend-Lease scheme before America's entry into World War II, and the trucks served with distinction in all theatres, including in the Soviet Union, which also received significant numbers. The 'Jimmy' made an enormous contribution to the Allied victory after the D-day landings by ensuring a reliable method of transport for supplies to units at the front, all of which had to be trucked across France until ports nearer Germany had been captured.

SPECIFICATIONS

COUNTRY OF ORIGIN: United States
CREW: 1
WEIGHT: 11,939kg (26,321lb)
DIMENSIONS: length 6.82m (22ft 4in); width 2.44m (8ft); height 3.01m (9ft 10in)
RANGE: 255km (158 miles)
ARMOUR: none
ARMAMENT: none
POWERPLANT: 1 x Hercules RXC 6-cylinder petrol engine developing 106hp (79kW)
PERFORMANCE: maximum road speed 64km/h (40mph); fording 0.75m (2ft 5in)

Austin 10

The Austin 10 Light Utility Truck was developed directly from a civilian vehicle, the Austin 10 Saloon. Made in the late 1930s, the truck was specifically for military use. It was made at the Austin Motor Co. in Birmingham. A small canvas-covered cargo area was added to the rear of the vehicle, suitable for carrying a payload of up to 250kg (550lb). Nicknamed the 'Tilly' after its official military designation 'Car, Light Utility, 4 x 2', the Austin 10 was ideal for staff duties, airfield duties and light ammunition carriage. Over 30,000 were produced during the war, recognizable by their angled front grille and cab-mounted spare wheel (though similar designs were produced by Standard, Hillman and Morris).

SPECIFICATIONS

COUNTRY OF ORIGIN: United Kingdom
CREW: 2
WEIGHT: 1003kg (2211lb)
DIMENSIONS: length 5.33m (17ft 5in); width 2.78m (9ft 1in); height 2.17m (7ft 1in)
RANGE: 190km (119 miles)
ARMOUR: none
ARMAMENT: none
POWERPLANT: 1 x Armstrong Siddeley 8-cylinder petrol, developing 90hp (67kW)
PERFORMANCE: maximum road speed: 35km/h (21mph)

Bedford OYC

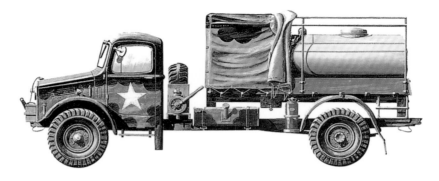

The Bedford OY was a 4 x 2 truck with a 3-ton load capacity. It became a mainstay of British forces during World War II. Based directly on a US 2½-ton truck design, the British appropriated the concept in 1940 in order to expedite development. The OY was a versatile, mass-produced truck capable of 80km/h (50mph). Bedford OYs cropped up in a bewildering array of variants. The OYC version shown here is a fuel carrier, the fuel containers shielded within a frame and tarpaulin cover, and a similar configuration was used to carry a 2046 litres (450 gal) water tank. A more unusual variant was a 4.3m (14ft 1in) unit, which contained X-ray facilities for use in battlefield medical emergencies.

SPECIFICATIONS
COUNTRY OF ORIGIN: United Kingdom
CREW: 2
WEIGHT: 7490kg (16,515lb) fully loaded
DIMENSIONS: length 6.22m (20ft 5in); width 2.17m (7ft 1in); height 3.1m (10ft 2in)
RANGE: 300km (186 miles)
ARMOUR: none
ARMAMENT: none
POWERPLANT: 1 x Bedford 6-cylinder petrol, developing 72hp (54kW)
PERFORMANCE: maximum road speed: 80km/h (50mph)

Bedford QLD

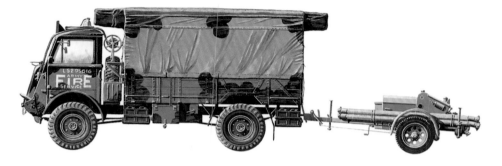

At the outbreak of World War II, Bedford was contracted by the British War Office to produce a 3-tonne 4 x 4 general service truck. The Bedford QLD was rapidly developed and the first production vehicles began to arrive in early 1941. Commendably, despite the speed of development, there were hardly any early problems with the vehicle. There were a number of variants on the basic design: the QLT troop carrier with room for 29 troops and kit, popularly known as the 'Drooper'; the QLR wireless truck; a vehicle adapted specifically to carry and fire the 6-pounder anti-tank gun from the body; and a fire tender. The Royal Air Force used them extensively as fuel tankers. An amphibious version – nicknamed the Giraffe – was developed but never passed the prototype stage.

SPECIFICATIONS

COUNTRY OF ORIGIN: United Kingdom
CREW: 1
WEIGHT: 12,727kg (26,998lb)
DIMENSIONS: length 5.99m (19ft 8in); width 2.26m (7ft 5in); height 3m (9ft 10in)
RANGE: 370km (230 miles)
ARMOUR: none
ARMAMENT: none
POWERPLANT: 1 x Bedford 6-cylinder petrol engine developing 72hp (53.7kW)
PERFORMANCE: maximum road speed 61km/h (38mph); fording 0.4m (1ft 4in)

TANKS AND ARMOURED VEHICLES 1900–1945 TRUCKS AND TRANSPORTERS

WEAPONS OF WAR

165

Mack 6 x 6

Mack was a well-established name in the truck manufacturing industry prior to World War II, and was thus well-placed to fulfil the transport needs of the US Army. The most prominent model produced, perhaps because of its size and power, was the Mack 6 x 6. This was mainly used by both British and American forces to tow heavy artillery pieces, such as the 155mm (6.1in) 'Long Tom' howitzers. The Canadians also used the truck widely for a variety of purposes. The truck was first seen in action in Italy. Despite their size, the Macks negotiated the difficult mountainous terrain to be at the forefront of the advance. The layout of the 6 x 6 was conventional, with the engine at the front, two-door cab in the centre with a fold-forward windscreen, and a cargo area at the rear.

SPECIFICATIONS

COUNTRY OF ORIGIN: United States
CREW: 1
WEIGHT: 19,813kg (43,588lb)
DIMENSIONS: length 7.54m (24ft 9in); width 2.62m (8ft 7in); height 3.15m (10ft 4in)
RANGE: 340km (211 miles)
ARMOUR: none
ARMAMENT: none
POWERPLANT: 1 x Mack EY 6-cylinder petrol engine developing 159hp (118.6kW)
PERFORMANCE: maximum road speed 84km/h (52.5mph); fording 0.76m (2ft 6in)

M5 High-Speed Tractor

Development of what was to become the M5 began in 1941 when the T20 and T21 were developed using the tracks and suspension of the M3 tank. In October 1942, the T21 was standardized as the M5, designed to tow 105mm (4.13in) and 155mm (6.1in) howitzers as well as their crew and equipment. Five different models were produced in all, differing mainly in their track and suspension. The vehicle entered production in 1942 and was built by International Harvester. A winch was fitted as standard and a roller under the winch allowed it to be used to pull vehicles to the front or to the rear. The vehicle did not outlast World War II by very long in the US Army, but it continued to serve with the armies of Austria, Japan, Yugoslavia and Pakistan for many years after 1945.

SPECIFICATIONS

COUNTRY OF ORIGIN: United States
CREW: 1 + 10
WEIGHT: 13,791kg (30,340lb)
DIMENSIONS: length 5.03m (16ft 6in); width 2.54m (8ft 4in); height 2.69m (8ft 10in)
RANGE: 241km (150 miles)
ARMOUR: none
ARMAMENT: 1 x 12.7mm (0.5in) Browning anti-aircraft machine gun
POWERPLANT: 1 x Continental R6572 6-cylinder petrol engine developing 207hp (154kW)
PERFORMANCE: maximum road speed 48km/h (30mph); fording 1.3m (4ft 4in); vertical obstacle 0.7m (2ft 3in); trench 1.7m (5ft 6in)

Raupenschlepper Ost

The Eastern Front presented the German Army with severe environmental challenges: deep snow in the winter and deep mud during the autumn rains and spring thaw. In 1942, the Raupenschlepper Ost (RSO) was developed to cope with these conditions. It was little more than a four-ton transport truck powered by a V-8 petrol engine, but fully tracked to handle demanding off-road terrain. Production began in 1943 under several manufacturers, and 27,000 units were produced by the end of the war. Its duties were varied, and included gun tractor, snow plough, trailer tractor and even ambulance. Two main versions were produced, the RSO/01 with a solid and enclosed cab, and the RSO/03, which had a soft-top cab.

SPECIFICATIONS

COUNTRY OF ORIGIN: Germany
CREW: 2
WEIGHT: 5200kg (11,464lb)
DIMENSIONS: length 4.42m (14ft 6in); width 1.99m (6ft 6in); height 2.53m (8ft 4in)
RANGE: 250km (155 miles)
ARMOUR: none
ARMAMENT: none
POWERPLANT: 1 x Steyr 1500A 8-cylinder petrol, developing 68hp (51kW)
PERFORMANCE: maximum road speed 17km/h (11mph)

Büssing-Nag

Germany relied heavily on modified civilian models for its heavy trucks when the war broke out as her rearmament programme was nowhere near completion. One of the types adapted was the Büssing-Nag 454 4 x 4 truck, designed to be used as a transporter unit for tanks. Only a small number were ever constructed as the 6 x 4 Faun was preferred for the role in most cases. Even this vehicle saw limited service as a tank-transport, as the German logistics system relied mainly on the railways for the movement of general supplies during World War II, with medium trucks taking on the task of distributing the equipment to the point of use. Heavy trucks were used most often for specialist roles such as carrying mobile radio stations for controlling armoured forces.

SPECIFICATIONS

COUNTRY OF ORIGIN: Germany
CREW: 1
WEIGHT: 9200kg (20,240lb)
DIMENSIONS: length 10.40m (34ft 1in); width 2.50m (8ft 2in); height 2.60m (8ft 6in)
RANGE: 270km (168 miles)
ARMOUR: none
ARMAMENT: none
POWERPLANT: 1 x Deutz F6M517 6-cylinder diesel engine developing 150hp (111.8kW)
PERFORMANCE: maximum road speed 65km/h (40.62mph); fording 0.4m (1ft 4in)

Chevrolet C60L

The Chevrolet C60L was one of the most numerous trucks built by the Canadians during World War II for supply to the British and other Commonwealth forces. This 3-ton 4 x 4 was a tremendously reliable vehicle, of sturdy yet simple design which allowed for rapid production. An enormous number of different models were produced including fuel tankers, ambulances and recovery vehicles. As well as different chassis, there was great differentiation in cab design as production progressed. For example, the number 13 cab was a complete redesign to allow more interior space and better positioning of the foot pedals. Other designs replaced the all-steel cab with a soft-top. The versatility of the range was remarkable and was reflected in the numbers in use.

SPECIFICATIONS

COUNTRY OF ORIGIN: Canada
CREW: 1
WEIGHT: 2100kg (4620lb)
DIMENSIONS: length 6.20m (20ft 4in); width 2.29m (7ft 6in); height 3.05m (10ft)
RANGE: 270km (168 miles)
ARMOUR: none
ARMAMENT: none
POWERPLANT: 1 x Ford V-8 petrol engine developing 95hp (71kW)
PERFORMANCE: maximum road speed 80km/h (50mph); fording 0.5m (1ft 7in)

Chevrolet WA

When the British found themselves unable to supply their own needs for vehicles in World War II, they turned to Canada for help. The Canadians had been working since 1937 on a standard truck based around a Ford V8 chassis. This 'Canadian Military Pattern Chassis' was to form the basis of many light and medium trucks supplied to Allied forces. Produced by both Ford and Chevrolet, the 4 x 4 was the mainstay of Canadian production through the war years. The Chevrolets were produced with either wood or steel bodies and used in an enormous number of roles, from ambulances to mobile gun carriages. Many were adapted for use by special forces such as the Long Range Desert Group in North Africa. Over 900,000 of all types of the basic chassis were produced before 1945.

SPECIFICATIONS

COUNTRY OF ORIGIN: Canada
CREW: 1
WEIGHT: 3048kg (6705lb)
DIMENSIONS: length 6.579m (21ft 7in); width 2.49m (8ft 2in); height 3m (9ft 9in)
RANGE: 274km (170 miles)
ARMOUR: none
ARMAMENT: 2 x machine guns, various calibres
POWERPLANT: 1 x Ford V-8 petrol engine developing 95hp (71kW)
PERFORMANCE: maximum road speed 80km/h (50mph); fording 0.5m (1ft 7in)

Krupp Kfz 81

The Kfz 81 was one of the most commonly used German light trucks during the early stages of World War II. The role in which it was most frequently seen was that of artillery tractor (it was the prime mover for the 20mm (0.79in) ant-aircraft gun), replacing the Kfz 69 purpose-built artillery tractor. The Kfz 81, or Krupp Boxer as it was known, had all-round independent suspension which allowed reasonable cross-country mobility. It was similar in many ways to contemporary six-wheeler British light trucks. In addition the indigenous light trucks, the Germans made extensive use of captured material such as the Czechoslovakian Tatra T92. Early German vehicles had stub axles amidships to carry the spare wheels, though there were never enough to go round even the élite field divisions.

SPECIFICATIONS

COUNTRY OF ORIGIN: Germany
CREW: 1
WEIGHT: 2600kg (5732lb)
DIMENSIONS: length 4.95m (16ft 3in); width 1.95m (6ft 5in); height 2.30m (7ft 7in)
RANGE: 300km (186 miles)
ARMOUR: none
ARMAMENT: none
POWERPLANT: 1 x Krupp M304 4-cylinder engine developing 52hp (38.8kW)
PERFORMANCE: maximum (rarely achieved) road speed 35km/h (21.75mph); fording not known; vertical obstacle 1.20m (3ft 8in); trench 2.59m (8ft 6in)

M29C Weasel

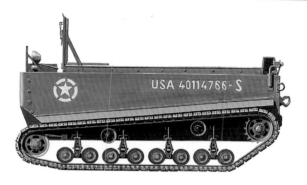

The M28 Weasel was developed for use by Allied commandos and special forces soldiers in northern European theatres. It was envisaged that raids against German heavy water plants in Norway could be conducted using small and fast oversnow vehicles. Even when that threat receded in 1942 after Norwegian partisan raids, production continued and the vehicles found use as light cargo carriers in Europe, the Pacific and Alaska. A fully amphibious version, the M29C, became the most popular version with over 15,000 units produced. The M29C had excellent mobility over snow, mud and soft sand, and could transport loads of 900kg (1990lb). After the war, some Scandinavian countries adapted the Weasel for civilian use.

SPECIFICATIONS
COUNTRY OF ORIGIN: United States
CREW: 1 + 3
WEIGHT: 1800kg (3968lb)
DIMENSIONS: length 4.79m (15ft 8in); width 1.7m (5ft 7in); height 1.82m (5ft 11in)
RANGE: 280km (174 miles)
ARMOUR: none
ARMAMENT: none
POWERPLANT: 1 x Studebaker Champion 6-170 6-cylinder petrol, developing 65hp (48kW) at 3600rpm
PERFORMANCE: maximum road speed: 58km/h (36mph); maximum water speed: 6km/h (4mph); fording: amphibious

Index